The Sq[

# SALTUS FIDELIS

## Lords & Kings

One man's quest to value these expressions, said in prayer to God: yet so alien to most Americans.

v2020-02-28

## Contents

Forward: This IS important! .................................................................... 4
   It's all true! ............................................................................................ 6
   But why Squirrels? ............................................................................... 7
   Of Reasons ............................................................................................ 8
(THURSDAY) ............................................................................................ 10
   Discussion 1: Fantasy and Faith. ..................................................... 11
   Discussion #2: No Room for honor ................................................ 16
   Discussion #2: (continued) ............................................................... 22
(FRIDAY) ................................................................................................... 24
   OF meaningless words ..................................................................... 24
   OF CIVIL DISOBEDIENCE .................................................................. 28
(SATURDAY) ............................................................................................ 38
   BUILDING BRIDGES FALLING DOWN .............................................. 38
(SUNDAY): ................................................................................................ 41
   MY LORD AND MY KING ................................................................... 43
   Casting down ...................................................................................... 47
(MONDAY) ............................................................................................... 56
   Of Small Vision ................................................................................... 56
(TUESDAY) ............................................................................................... 61
   Of Lords ............................................................................................... 61
(Wednesday) ........................................................................................... 69
(THURSDAY) ............................................................................................ 78
   Of Commoners and Kings ................................................................ 82

v2020-02-28

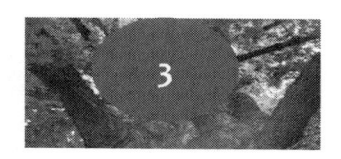

(FRIDAY) .................................................................... 94
    Of Governors and Presidents. ................................. 98
    Subjects or Subjugated? ........................................ 103
TODAY: Peace in Chaos ............................................. 109
    Appendix: the BACKGROUND of the book ............. 110
Index ............................................................................ 117
Index ............................................................................ 118
Bibliography ................................................................. 119
Your Memoirs .............................................................. 120

## Forward: This IS important!

# "Thy Kingdom Come, Thy Will be Done."

*The American Revolution, The French Revolution, The Russian Revolution*; Each time a people and a generation declare their national distrust and anger at their Lord and King.

They create documents and declarations to never allow another king to arise to govern their society, and constitutions to confirm that they will never again be ruled by a monarchy.

Yes, it is true, that a few nations maintain a national pride and joy in their historical monarchy but there are very few actually being ruled by such. The majority of nations who keep a rich heritage of a royalty, maintain them as revered figureheads, while adopting representative or other forms of governments

In the rise of the Entertainment media, we design our own historical kings and lords. We are presented with caricatures of villains, or with mighty men who age, demonstrate some terrible weakness, and pass away, or buffoons who we can ridicule in cartoons and comedy.

Every step takes us farther and farther from accurately imagining or desiring God's Kingdom to appear on Earth.

We pray for the return of His Kingdom, we repeatedly refer to Him as Lord, without having the vaguest idea of what it means to be a subject within a kingdom, or to be a vassal of a Lord. Can we flippantly use these words without considering how it should impact our whole way of thinking?

This book, and the conversations between the characters, are designed to promote two things in your heart.

A rich and complete desire for a king and kingdom in your life that exists on Earth as it is in Heaven.

A right relationship with a Lord, your Lord, who you may come to follow with desire and delight.

## IT'S ALL TRUE!

"The most important words are these: 'Hear, Oh Peoples! The Lord our God, the Lord is one.

What has always stood out to me, emotionally and spiritually was the word "GOD". But lately I have given a lot of consideration to what I was missing. In front of me, twice, was the word: "LORD". I have a working understanding of GOD, but I never really appreciated, understood or valued the concept of "LORD".

**To keep this command without spot or blame until the appearing of our Lord Jesus Christ, which God will bring about in his own time—God, the blessed and only Ruler, the KING OF KINGS and Lord of lords, who alone is immortal and who lives in unapproachable light, whom no one has seen or can see.** -an excerpt from Paul of Tarsus to his student Timothy, circa AD 63

Here again, the words that would catch my attention would be 'God, Unseen, Jesus' and 'Unapproachable Light' because these were all concepts that were familiar to me. Yet, somehow, I continued to gloss over 'Lord' and 'King' in the same sentence. Having little emotional ties to KING or LORD, I yearn to know what does this all mean?

The need to understand, to have a LORD and KING in my life is very true, very real. The story, of course, is storytelling.

v2020-02-28

## BUT WHY SQUIRRELS?
I suppose you may wonder why I chose squirrels to deliver the messages of this story? The answer is simple. It was the easiest path to begin with. I had already written three fantasy books in a series called "The Squirrels of Saltus Fidelis", and within those books I had created all the settings, places, characters and creatures that I needed.

This is not a child's book. This is intended for mature audiences, as the material that is covered will challenge the mature thinker. The actors, that is the squirrels, do not act immature or childish, but act with a level of insight, decorum and maturity that is lacking in many gatherings today.

All three of the previous volumes are well suited for both youth and mature audiences, with several insights woven into each story.

I suppose I could have used Elves, Dragons, beings of light, Aliens from outer space, or prophets from the past, but then I would be tasked with developing their backstories, and all the literary pieces that I already had developed in the Squirrels of Saltus Fidelis.

So, if you particularly don't much like squirrels, you have my permission to, as you read, to supplement the characters with character types such as "elves" or "aliens" or "prophets" or whatever works best for you.

## OF REASONS
I have written, thus far, three volumes about the beautiful land of Saltus Fidelis, a land that I have been privileged to visit on many occasions. As you are aware, if you have read my earlier accounts, Saltus Fidelis is a world, mostly invisible to our own, that through a great misfortune impacted with our Earth nearly 5,000 years ago.

And now, Saltus Fidelis in the realm of fantasy, and Earth, in the realm of physics, rotate and twirl around each other, locked together like two battling tops.

What had led up to this visit (the one detailed in this book), was that, only moments before, I had left my Wednesday evening bible study with fellow believers, followers of Jesus. During our closing moments we sang a few praise songs about our wonderful Lord and King Jesus. Someone concluded our time with a prayer, interjecting, as I often would, the word, 'Lord' before each sentence or phrase.

As I sat thinking after the meeting: What is a Lord. What is a King?
I knew that I was asking an important question that I had no answer to.
As an American, Connecticut Yankee, our history was born out of the rejection of a Monarchy, and the oppression that is built into the monarchy system upon its subjects.

v2020-02-28

The men who framed our declaration of independence were seeking to escape one Monarchy, and then, through our constitution, prevent a monarchy from ever taking root in our country.

Yet, every time I prayed, I would beg my King, Father God, for His Kingdom to come on Earth as it is in Heaven. I would call him my Lord, just as one would do in any Monarchial system. What I claimed to want for in Eternity was the exact opposite of what I would accept in my life.

Somehow, I knew the kingdom of Saltus Fidelis, a land that I had written three volumes about, a land that was intensely good, and a land that was one hundred percent, a monarchy would help me understand.
And Perhaps, if I could understand how the Lords of Saltus Fidelis receive their power, how they dispense their duties, and why they are so loved by their citizenry, then I might value my own Lord in the way that I really wish that I could.
Likewise, for Kings, If I could understand the nature, power and authority; the majesty and benevolence of a King, perhaps I could value my Heavenly King in the way that I know that I ought to.

## (THURSDAY)

As I was travelling to the portal to take me back to Saltus Fidelis, I knew that I would be documenting my entire journey, the physical, moral and spiritual aspects. But I was not sure how to certify that my readers would have enough background knowledge of Saltus Fidelis and its inhabitants to understand all the nuances of the story.

If I placed all the background in the front of the book, I discovered that it would add nearly 30 pages of reading that really did not have anything to do with the subject. So, after much consideration, I added all the historical, demographic and story context to the end of this book.

As I returned to Saltus Fidelis, the first thought to pique my interest was that, rather than each of the individual races of creatures and inhabitants unifying and creating their own sovereign systems, (something that by law is both permitted and encouraged to do at any time) all inhabitants and races prefer and willingly swear their allegiance and fealty to the One monarchy that rules Saltus Fidelis.

There was no need to question how well this worked, for I had seen the government of Saltus Fidelis with my own eyes, and the immutable love of all citizens for the royal family.

Even in the past, this caused me to do a little personal soul searching, since I knew that when I prayed, I often addressed my words to "Lord Jesus" and I would call God, or Jesus my "King", yet honestly, those terms were somewhat empty and anti-climactic to a Connecticut Yankee.

And so, I came this time to Saltus Fidelis seeking answers about their religion, about Lordship, and being a citizen of a kingdom.

**DISCUSSION 1: FANTASY AND FAITH.**
My first meeting of the week would be hastily arranged, with Taelbaerer, the great grey sage Squirrel, standing at 4.5 feet tall, who welcomed me to his cottage home, carefully hewn from a large tree.

Even though I had visited Saltus Fidelis many times, Taelbaerer knew that this visit was different, I was seeking truth and knowledge, and not just to tag along on adventures.

Taelbaerer was eager, as is the way of squirrels, to discuss with me the principles of Fantasy and Faith.

Taelbaerer began by reciting a poem, the first in his salvo of explanations.

*God is one.*
*There is no God besides Him.*

*But the World believes only*
*what they can see,*
*what they can create.*
*There is no Faith*
*in the One who created all.*
*And so, to grow a yearning*
*for believing in that which is not seen*
*The world was given Fantasy*
*and storytellers.*

*Then you may allow storytelling*
*of gods, Lyrids, fairies,*
*and powerful battles between good and evil.*
*And outgrowing Fantasy,*
*Faith grows in the one Great God.*


With a brief pause to let the poem sink in to me, Taelbaerer continued his explanation:
"It is difficult to nearly impossible to believe in factual stories of truthful wonder, such as
> *the power of the Highest shall overshadow you:*
> *therefore also that holy thing which shall be born*
> *of you shall be called the Son of God.,*

and
> *And Jesus was transfigured before them: and his*
> *face shined like the sun, and his clothing was*
> *white as light itself.*

Taelbaerer continued:
"I can show you hundreds more "Truthful Wonders" which you accept as true, but often fail to appreciate. For someone like yourself, who have learned to use your imagination, it is possible that you understand. Sadly, for others, words remain as dry and unexciting as the ingredients on a bottle of hand cleaner. Then Taelbaerer handed me an easily recognizable reprint of a picture of the face of Jesus, bleeding and covered in thorns. And as he prepared to read, Taelbaerer said, "Please, "Novinaja, is this how you limit your picture of your God? Can you see what I am about to read? These are real pictures of your King in Heaven!

> *I saw the Lord, high and exalted, seated on a throne; and the train of his robe filled the temple. Above him were seraphim, each with six wings: With two wings they covered their faces, with two they covered their feet, and with two they were flying. And they were calling to one another: "Holy, holy, holy is the LORD Almighty; the whole earth is full of his glory. At the sound of their voices the doorposts and thresholds shook and the temple was filled with smoke.*

As Taelbaerer continued to read, I heard him saying to himself aloud, "Our One Great God is no more intimidated by Dormammu, Thanos, any of the celestials or eternals, any more than He was intimidated by Ra, Osiris, Set or Horus. If only these people would imagine their God having all these pyrotechnic powers!".

## 14

Then Taelbaerer Read:

> *I looked, and I saw a windstorm coming out of the north— an immense cloud with flashing lightning and surrounded by brilliant light. The center of the fire looked like glowing metal, and in the fire was what looked like four living creatures. In appearance their form was human, but each of them had four faces and four wings.*
>
> *When the creatures moved, I heard the sound of their wings, like the roar of rushing waters, like the voice of the Almighty, like the tumult of an army. When they stood still, they lowered their wings.*
>
> *Then there came a voice from above the vault over their heads as they stood with lowered wings.*
>
> *Above the vault over their heads was what looked like a throne of lapis lazuli, and high above on the throne was a figure like that of a man.*
>
> *I saw that from what appeared to be his waist up he looked like glowing metal, as if full of fire, and that from there down he looked like fire; and brilliant light surrounded him.*
>
> *Like the appearance of a rainbow in the clouds on a rainy day, so was the radiance around him. This was the appearance of the likeness of the glory of the LORD. When I saw it, I fell facedown, and I heard the voice of one speaking.*

"To the maturing mind, yearning for the unseen, "; Taelbaerer concluded, "that have grown up with fantasy and fables, a God shaped hole in their own heart opens wide, and they long for the unseen God to fill it."

Several days later, Taelbaerer handed me a scroll. I opened it, noted its author and date, smiled and handed it back to Taelbaerer. Taelbaerer handed it to a young assistant squirrel with a lovely voice who read it to us whilst we sipped on our tea.

## DISCUSSION #2: NO ROOM FOR HONOR

*"Is the march of events ordered and guided by eminent men, or do our leaders merely fall into their places at the heads of the moving columns? ...*
*if this be true of the daily experience of ordinary average people, how much more potent must be the deflection which the Master Teachers, Thinkers, Discoverers, Commanders have imparted at every stage. True, they require their background, their atmosphere, their opportunity;*

*Is not mankind already escaping from the control of individuals? Are not our affairs increasingly being settled by mass processes? Are not modern conditions at any rate throughout the English-speaking communities hostile to the development of outstanding personalities and to their influence upon events: and lastly if this be true, will it be for our greater good and glory? These questions merit some examination from thoughtful people. Certainly, we see around us today a marked lack of individual leadership.*

*It must be admitted that in one great sphere the thrones are neither vacant nor occupied by pygmies. Science in all its forms surpasses itself every year. The body of knowledge ever accumulating is immediately interchanged and the quality and fidelity of the research never flags.*

*But here again the mass effect largely suppresses the individual achievement. The throne is occupied; but by a throng.*

*We have long seen the old family business, where the master was in direct personal touch with his workmen, swept out of existence or absorbed by powerful companies, which in their turn are swallowed by mammoth trusts.*

*The newspapers do an immense amount of thinking for the average man and woman. In fact, they supply them with such a continuous stream of standardized opinion, borne along upon an equally inexhaustible flood of news and sensation, collected from every part of the world every hour of the day, that there is neither the need nor the leisure for personal reflection.*

*Modern conditions do not lend themselves to the production of the heroic or super-dominant type. On the whole they are fatal to pose. "*
    *Sir Winston Churchill,    1925*
    *The mass effects of modern life.*

I looked up and understood that we would begin on the notion that my race has not only forgotten how to honor Individuals, but that honoring individuals has become counter-cultural, and possibly even bad for cultural advancement. I perceived that maybe this would cause us to become poor students at understanding Nobles and Kings.

I remember once when I had just returned to Saltus Fidelis after 3 years back home in Connecticut, USA.  All I could talk about was how happy I was to be back in a country where laws and government made sense, because back in my home, everything and everyone was broken.  I remember moaning to Taelbaerer that all of my elected leaders are fools, and there may be good leaders, but those that lead are good for nothing.

I ranted on and on about the evils of my worthless government, until I noticed Taelbaerer's tail twitching in pure disgust.

"My dear friend", he said, "Peace!  It is obvious that some singular event has happened, and now you are beside yourself in torturous anger.  What was the event, may I ask?"

I took a long and sheepish breath, "You are correct, and I apologize for my ranting. I am upset for one event, and have assigned my anger of that event toward any and every person even remotely associated".

Taelbaerer just stood there, waiting for me.

I continued "There's to be a vote to raise taxes on products that I buy all the time. If it passes, I'll have to adjust my budget again"

Taelbaerer frowned, lowered his tail and continued: "Ah, let me read you something."

And Taelbaerer opened a larger scroll that seemed older and more precious to him. Again he handed it to the young squirrel scribe to read it to both of us:

## DISCUSSION #2: (CONTINUED)

*Let everyone be subject to the governing authorities, for there is no authority except that which God has established.*

*The authorities that exist have been established by God. Consequently, whoever rebels against the authority is rebelling against what God has instituted, and those who do so will bring judgment on themselves.*

*For rulers hold no terror for those who do right, but for those who do wrong.*

*Do you want to be free from fear of the one in authority?*

*Then do what is right and you will be commended.*

*For the one in authority is God's servant for your good.*

*But if you do wrong, be afraid, for rulers do not bear the sword for no reason.*

*They are God's servants, agents of wrath to bring punishment on the wrongdoer.*

*Therefore, it is necessary to submit to the authorities, not only because of possible punishment but also as a matter of conscience.*

*This is also why you pay taxes, for the authorities are God's servants, who give their full time to governing.*

*Give to everyone what you owe them:*

*If you owe taxes, pay taxes;*

*if revenue, then revenue;*

*if respect, then respect;*

*if honor, then honor.*

Then, it seemed as though Taelbaerer was ranting on me!

"Novinaja, tell me, how can something this sappily written 2,000 years ago apply to YOUR modern civilization? The person who dared to write such folly, whose meager life experiences of living during the tumultuous time of YOUR insane Caesar Nero, certainly could not qualify him to give you and your fellow men and women social-political advice today. Just like his antiquated ideas on women wearing hats in church, you certainly have the right to ignore this passage also."

Then wrapping his tail around my neck and pulling my head toward his face, as he leaned in, he said in a stern voice, pronouncing each word with an intensity I had not seen before:

"Or - do - we?"

The sermon on the previous page, is an excerpt from a much longer letter written by Paul (Saul of Tarsus) to the community of Jewish and Gentile believers in Jesus. Romans (Romans 13:1-7).

v2020-02-28

(FRIDAY)

## OF MEANINGLESS WORDS

Since the study of these documents were at the core of my fascination with Saltus Fidelis, and its benevolent, but unmistakably all-powerful Monarchy, I requested a private audience of Taelbaerer to discuss these documents, and the Kingdom, with possibly discourteous probing into the care and cultivation of the populace, and the management or squelching of dissention.

Although Taelbaerer was annoyed at my almost intentional forgetfulness, he was nevertheless unshaken in his desire to make me his student.

So Taelbaerer opened a much more recent book, one that he had ordered from Amazon. I recognized it immediately. It was the first book that I penned on the subject of the History of Saltus Fidelis.

He flipped to page 96, and reminded me that although Saltus Fidelis has a class system, it is a "class system" only in the sense that a 1st grade student and an adult earning their MBA are in different classes.

"But so far, everything that I have written is so superficial" I pleaded with Taelbaerer, "Why isn't there a single dissenter in your nation? Why don't I ever hear of the citizens harboring plots in secret?

v2020-02-28

Why don't the other Lords of Saltus Fidelis ever meet with all their nobles to take counsel together, against unjust and unfair practices or laws of your own lord and King and the High council?

Smiling at my thinly veiled use of biblical references, and stroking his long tail in a manner that only this Taelbaerer knows how to perform, he replied,

"Ask them yourself,", replied Taelbaerer, " I am sure that they would enjoy a good laugh"

A slow chuckle arose in Taelbaerer's tail, and although I felt it in my belly too, I did not know if I was being laughed at, or laughed with.

But I shall focus on the singular topic which is greater than all, "continued Taelbaerer, and then he paused for a while, as if searching for his next word, but his next word was simply: **"Words."**

Taelbaerer began:
"Your Earth used to value words.  Words had power. You mysteriously enjoyed acknowledging that your savior was the express WORD of the ONE GREAT GOD, without having any reasonable attachment to the concept of "WORDS".

"If your Earth grasped words in the same way that our One Great God does, or, at least in the same way that we at Saltus Fidelis do."

"Let's look at these documents that you brought to me."

At that, Taelbaerer took the second parchment, my copy of the letter of Paul of Tarsus to the followers of Jesus in Rome, and scanned it over again.

He sat silently for over an hour.

Then Taelbaerer spoke again.
"To repeat the words of your Paul of Tarsus to the citizens in Saltus Fidelis – they would wonder why someone would have written such a list of frivolous laws and ordinances, for these words are as irrelevant as 'don't forget to breath, or don't forget to swallow'".

"In our land our words, our promises have meaning, and having meaning, they have value, and having value, they have eminent domain over all else in our life."

v2020-02-28

Taelbaerer continued.

"Therefore, if any citizen, from the most noble Fox or Squirrel to the basest of all pigeons or antelope, should speak a promise to a spouse, an employer, or a pledge of allegiance to a cause or country, their words are incontrovertible, unassailable, and immutable because they are purposed in their heart.

"But what about your letter from Paul of Tarsus to the Christians in Rome? I am curious," continued Taelbaerer, "do your people laugh boisterously when they read this passage?"

"There is one point here that I must clarify the stance of Saltus Fidelis. Whereas Paul writes "whoever rebels against the authority is rebelling against what God has instituted" we have nationally interpreted the "whoever" to be individuals or small groups of anarchists. The laws of Saltus Fidelis allow two specific ordinances which may or may not agree with your own interpretation of Paul's writings:"

> "First, A fully represented group of persons, in order to create a sovereign nation, may peacefully or by other means secure itself as a sovereign nation within a territory once held by another sovereign nation. Yes, this has always been an offer of Saltus Fidelis to all her inhabitants, but none have shown desire.
>
> Second, any sovereign nation may invade the borders of another adjacent sovereign land in order to establish peace and morality within the whole land."

## OF CIVIL DISOBEDIENCE
*(AKA, the oldest Sin in the book)*

At this point, Taelbaerer had grasped the end strands of his tail, and twisting them, made it into a type of a pointer stick. Holding his large tail, and thick pointer like end between me and his face, I felt very much on the hotseat, grilled as it were, by a squirrel.

Taelbaerer pushed on, as I squirmed in my seat, "Civil Obedience! That is the focal point to everything that you are seeking to understand. You wonder 'why is there no civil disobedience', but our philosophy which you find difficult to believe is that 'a society of civil <u>obedience</u> is the preferred and better state of all creatures'".

After a brief pause to pour us both some delicious Hazelnut blend coffee, Taelbaerer continued: "None of this should surprise you. What was the One Great God's first and only requirement upon creating your world?

I thought for a moment,
"Obedience?" I asked


Civil disobedience was being promoted by pen and thinker long before your Paul suggested Civil Obedience could work amongst the world of men."

v2020-02-28

Taelbaerer continued: "From the foundations of your people, your earth mother was enticed into an act of civil disobedience against God, simply by doing an action that she was told never to do.  It has been written into your DNA ever since.

Even Aristotle wrote: "*It is not always the same thing to be a good man and a good citizen.*"

"And prominent and highly revered statesmen and women continue to promote *Civil Disobedience, WHEN NECESSARY, as necessary.* "

Then he handed me a list of quotations, I focused on two, which read:

Alexaksandr Solzhenitzn wrote, "*Let us put it generally: if a regime is immoral, its subjects are free from all obligations to it.*"

Henry David Thoreau wrote, "*Disobedience is the true foundation of liberty. The obedient must be slaves.*"

Taking a deep breath, Taelbaerer continued:
"There is *another* law, a much higher law, of civil obedience that appears on the surface like civil disobedience, but it is not. It is the law of The KING OF KINGS.",

Taking another sip of tea, he continued,

"all rulers and leaders are subject to the authority given to them by the KING OF KINGS, namely the Highest God and His Son Jesus. If an individual is forced to choose between the law of a king, ruler or governor, and the law of the KING OF KINGS, it is NOT the individual who is committing an act of civil disobedience; *it is the king, ruler or governor who is in full disobedience to the KING OF KINGS.*

Even if a law is a written code but that code is in disobedience to the KING OF KINGS, the Law of the KING OF KINGS supersedes. The one who obeys the KING OF KINGS law, while disregarding illegal codes and statutes is guiltless before God and His Son Jesus.

A popular example, which is often tossed about and misinterpreted as individuals who were followers of the Lord Jesus committing lawless acts of civil disobedience is when, as recorded by Doctor Luke circa 62 AD in the following legal proceeding:

v2020-02-28

## Case Study: Historian Dr Luke. Acts52529

A concerned citizen reported to the authorities: "Look! The prisoners have escaped and are already defying the court gag-order ACT418 from further commenting on the matters of this trial!"

Immediately, the district attorney and a large contingent of the police unit convinced the Jesus followers to return with them without any violence, fearing an outbreak of riots.

The men were brought in to appear before a panel of religious and judicial authorities, and to be interrogated by the High Court.

"We gave you a strict gag-order not to teach or discuss matters about the name of the man that you were following during the past several years, yet you have broadcast your stories throughout this our city, Jerusalem.

Not only that, but I'll have you know that several of us are charging you with slander, because you accuse us of murdering an innocent man.

The followers of Jesus then replied "We must obey God rather than human beings!"

As you can see, Novinaja, said Taelbaerer, Not only was ACT418 an illegal order against the Law of the King of Kings, but the men were not acting in civil disobedience, but on complete obedience to the law of the King of Kings.

" Taelbaerer then asked me?
"You look perplexed?"

I was quite dumbfounded, after a while I was able to say a few disjointed thoughts.

I asked:
"I am, I am quite confused. Would you say that even our American Revolution was an act of Civil Disobedience?"

Taelbaerer was quick to reply,
"It rode on the backs of many acts of civil disobedience. Incidents celebrated by your country as heroic men, were considered mere bands of rioters by the leaders of the country of what was then your king."

I continued to press the point:
"But you said that even within Saltus Fidelis, you recognize the right of an organized succession and formation of a new nation"

Taelbaerer replied:
"Yes, The day that your delegates convened to write that sacred scroll, the American Declaration of Independence", you gained the right and became a new nation under heaven.
However, even in your Declaration document, the prize of an individual's right to civil disobedience in the face of any law flowed from your personal DNA into the DNA of your nation. Like a virus, the law of civil disobedience has now become one of the most protected rights in your country"

I moved onto another subject,
 "and you had said earlier that this somehow was affecting my relationship with God?", I pleaded

Taelbaerer replied, "From the moment you get into your car, you will often, almost immediately begin breaking the laws of your country. Yet you will feel no guilt or remorse because you are protected by the superior law of Group Civil Disobedience (everyone does it), and intellectual civil disobedience (I would be a hazard to others by driving the speed limit).

Taelbaerer's tail and voice was becoming quite stern as he continued:
"But just as I have seen how your people applaud and celebrate dissidents, I am also certain that you have taken this stance before the One Great God.
You feel the freedom to declare to the One Great God that Civil disobedience to HIM is not always sin.
And when, what you personally believe of His nature, intellectually contradicts with His written word, you say that you can prove your interpretations are correct, because you understand historical references, ancient languages, or something like that.
Then you ask to be applauded and celebrated, and go off and write books about it.

"For example, my dear boy," Taelbaerer's voice and tail now softened as he continued, as though he was talking to his young student squirrels and not an old man from Earth. Nevertheless, I always appreciated his caring nature. "For example, you are able to remove any part of your New Testament ordinances and warnings by telling your God, not to his face, mind you, only a few would do that, but definitely in your heart, that either 'the group laws of civil disobedience', or the 'intellectual laws of civil disobedience supersede any word from your Lord."

"You believe that Group civil disobedience defends you when you are tempted to redefine roles of men and women in marriage, in the family, in the church, and the community. And how it also defends you when you see need, or the opportunity to talk about your personal hope, and you withhold your charity, simply because it is the norm."

"But you also believe that intellectual civil disobedience protects you by allowing you to determine which biblical teachings are culturally passé, which are so vague that there is no valid interpretation, or which only applied to a certain type group or type of people, but not to you. For your convenience every generation will list some of Paul's writings regarding lifestyles as culturally antiquated, and others as immutable and permanent."

Because I was not looking at Taelbaerer at this moment, I did not see the twitch of an ironic smile form through his tail and face, as one would have after revealing a clever joke:
"If I made wooden signs for humans, I would want to make them more truthful, such as 'Love your God, with all your mind, all your heart and all your soul, except when the laws of civil disobedience allow you to do none of the above"

"Taelbaerer", I asked with my face cupped in my hands, "I do not understand what all this talk of Civil disobedience has to do with my ability to learn about the reality of a Lord and a King in my own life"

For the first time Taelbaerer exhibited signs of dismay. "It has everything to do with it! It is the hinge, the very fulcrum between never appreciating your Lord and King, and fully giving yourself to your Lord and King without loss or pain."

Taelbaerer continued: "Do you remember that James asked: **How can you love God that you do not see and hate your brother that you do see**? Well, It is the very same. How can you obey and honor God that you do not see, when you will not obey or honor the authorities that He has placed over you that you do see on Earth?"

v2020-02-28

"Do you recall two situations where your Lord Jesus talked about those who called him Lord without indulging in what they were saying? Your Lord Jesus asked, **'Why do you call me, Lord, Lord, and do not do what I say?'**

And at another time your Lord Jesus was telling a story about those who supposed that they were His Followers, found themselves asking Jesus as he was pronouncing sentence upon them **"Begone from my sight, for I was naked and you did not clothe me, hungry and you did not feed me, in prison and you did not visit me?"** and the followers replied **"Lord, when did we see you in need and do nothing about it?"**

"Do you not understand, the crusades of civil disobedience that you take up on earth resonate on your heavenly capacity to obey or call Jesus your Lord or King!"

"Don't play yourself the fool. If I am going to train you how to love a Lord who loved you first, you must lay aside any exit strategy of your right of civil disobedience"

I sat there pondering the many responses that I could make. On one hand, I could justify myself, explaining that he knew nothing of the human condition, nor of the need for truly good men to dispel tyrants, and to overcome bad laws and leaders, yes, even by force if necessary.
I could explain that his overuse of 'civil disobedience' were based on his viewpoints of right and wrong; and his interpretation of God's laws; and how dare he judge me.

But somehow, I really did not want to argue at all. For the first time in my life, I gave way to the humility of pondering over all of what had been said.

Now Taelbaerer's demeanor softly changed. You can always perceive the mood of any squirrel, first in their tail. It is an instant clue on how they are feeling. The tail, and the fur of the tail may be relaxed, or stiff, shake or vibrate, or sway softly. Now Taelbaerer reminded me of the most important news that I had almost forgotten, after all this discussion on civil disobedience. It was the Good News itself.
Taelbaerer, changed his position from leaning into my face, being a hard schoolmaster, to an observant friend. He leaned back, and surveyed me for a while, waiting for me to speak.

Finally, Taelbaerer broke the silence: "My dear friend. Your own Paul wrote about this human condition by saying **that 'All have used the laws of civil disobedience to offend Gods, and explain their actions, in doing so they have fallen short of the Glory of the one great God.' And again 'even when everyone was in full civil disobedience, Jesus Died for us'".**
One of the most wonderful spiritual truths is the Salvation Story of Humans, a story unique to you and to your kind, filled with more wonderous belief than Saltus Fidelis itself.

"You have received a gift that many of you do not want because you do not understand your need, that we want more than all the acorns under heaven, but cannot have because we do not need!"

v2020-02-28

## (SATURDAY)

### BUILDING BRIDGES FALLING DOWN

The next morning, as I made my way up the path to Taelbaerer's humble abode, the weight of the previous day's conversation seemed to become a very real set of shackles, chains and iron balls dragging behind me. Every step was now a trudge.

I was already visualizing Taelbaerer waiting for me, ready to splay open my spiritual hypocrisy - my eagerness to have a God, but keep my safety net of cultural wisdom and not live in complete obedience to Him.

As I entered the door of Taelbaerer's house, I encountered the unexpected.

Before me set a brightly adorned breakfast table, filled with the best foods of Saltus Fidelis. Red meat is of course an oxymoron, stress the moron, on Saltus Fidelis, but fish is not. (I asked about this once to a lively low herald squirrel who was seated next to me at a great feast years ago, and all she could squeak out was "If the Savior of Earth could have a fish fry on the beach with the boys after he rose from the dead, we figure its good enough for us". Due to the 1 hour and 30 minutes of squirrel laugher that followed, I have never asked that question again.) I have arrived in my drabbest student's uniform, expecting to be reamed again for humankind's hypocrisy in what they say and act.

v2020-02-28

But clearly Taelbaerer had other ideas on where to take our conversation today.

"Novinaja, my dear friend", began Taelbaerer, sitting directly across from me, sipping on his morning coffee (which he often spiked with the pure nectar of Hazelnut trees, 'stimulating without inebriating' he would often tell me").

"I am so delighted to see that you have returned", declared Taelbaerer.

"I am not sorry that you had to endure the tearing away of the hard-outer shell that prevented access to your heart and mind. That is why my questions of late to you have been so harsh."

"But I have been acting on the desires of Saltus Fidelis.

I changed both my physical and emotional position in the beautiful hand-carved oak chair which, for the first time, I noticed that although being all wood, it was of utmost comfort.

v2020-02-28

"Even though you know so much about our nation, to answer your questions about our faith and religion, you would have to learn about our kingdom, which to date, you have thought of in terms as quaint or feudal.

"You have carried with you a preconceived bias that all creatures must exist in a passion of civil-disobedience, because the opposite of civil disobedience must be, in your philosophy, only state-control and manipulative dictatorship.

"Are you willing, for the sake of your mission, to abandon this bias completely?

If I had answered no, then there would have been no book for you to read, dear reader, so it should be obvious to you that I immediately answered "YES".

"Very good," replied Taelbaerer, "Please enjoy your day today, there should be no Earth-shadow to limit your exercise, but also do try to get in a nap before our meeting this evening. You will need to be well rested.

## (SUNDAY):

"Wake up!" a sharp stinging bite on my toe, and the shrill voice of the tiny low herald squirrel finally had me back from my odd dreams, which were so real as I was dreaming, but the memory of which vanished the instant I woke up.

I often wonder how that could be so, how you can live so vividly in a dream, and wake up and instantly forget all the characters and all the conversations that were just seconds ago so vital and life-shattering.

On a prior visit years ago, I had visited the great public library of Saltus Fidelis, where the inscription "ego eram in somnio papilionem" is engraved in 4-foot-high letters. It is the first stanza of the very ancient proverb, first attributed to the Chinese Philosopher, Zhuangzi, around 290 BC, but more likely found in the Annals of Saltus Fidelis another 400 years earlier by Taelbaerer The Seafarer circa 683 Earth BCE.
The full poem goes (Saltus Fidelis Version)

>I dreamed I was a butterfly,
>then I awoke.
>Now I wonder:
>Am I that which I perceive that I am now,
>who dreamt of being a butterfly,
>or am I a butterfly dreaming,
>merely perceiving of who I think I am now?

v2020-02-28

42

As Taelbaerer explained even on my prior visits, I must never close my mind to the possibilities of the unexplained and to allow that which seems "impossible" to have residency in my mind and heart.

"WAKE UP!" Another sharp bite on the toe, as I apparently dozed off, musing about dreams.
"You are to come with me, we shall meet King Tomek. It is your time for you to give your presentation to the council"

## MY LORD AND MY KING

I have been to the great council of Saltus Fidelis on many occasions, but always as an observer and journalist. It was unthinkable that I could be a participant. I had no skill to give at the tail-fluffing.

All of that was changing soon.

I found that Taelbaerer had the seamstress squirrels working tirelessly, for there before me was a gentlemen's outfit that would be appropriate for any English Court, regardless of the century or event.

I entered the great hall of the Great Council of Saltus Fidelis, and was amazed how much larger it appeared from the center, than from the upper sides, where I had always stood and reported from.

On the well maintained perfectly round floor of polished and sparkling golden wood which was the bottom level of the auditorium, stood three tables, each with 4 chairs, although each had room for a 5th chair.

v2020-02-28

The missing space, was always in the position of what would have been the middle chair, or 3rd chair counting from either end. And at the space was a plaque which had the inscription and likeliness of Peggy, High Herald Squirrel.

> *"and as she entered squirrel's Blessed*
> *"She knew her mission had passed the test"*

Taelbaerer was waiting for me at the center table. I sat next to him, to the right of the Peggy seat. The left of the Peggy seat would sit the low herald who escorted me and a chipmunk whom I had come to find out, was shadowing me every minute since I arrived at Saltus Fidelis.

The right and left tables were empty for now.
I was facing an elevated stage, raised about 5 levels up, with one long and very ornate table, at least from what I could see of its front. There were 10 Chairs.
To each side were the entrances to each level, that began each level of seating. Behind me, there was a semi-arc, which was tiered for about 30 levels of auditorium seating, divided by level aisles and causeways.

I surmised that the brightly colored carpets were used throughout to quickly guide each animal group to their kinsfolk and voting segments.

The entire auditorium was hewn out of the conjoined trunks of several oak trees.

Immediately after I sat down, Taelbaerer turned to watch as hordes of squirrel delegates and participants filled the chamber. Taking my cue from Taelbaerer, I too watched intently.
Next came the delegates of the Chipmunks, Rabbits and Possums. All These seem to fill up to the lower 20 levels.
Then entered the delegates from all of the remaining animal races living in Saltus Fidelis, mice, skunk, bluebird, pigeon, stork, horse, deer, racoon, and thousands of other species.

The events proceeded quickly, and the delegates seemed to police themselves, and calm down quickly and prepare for the next step.

As soon as there was complete silence in the Auditorium, several columns of Praetorium Guard Squirrels, all dressed in their Military finest, Filed in up to 6 rows deep in front of the stage.

In scurried, 9 squirrels, wearing the full royal outfits of the court. I should explain "scurried". Their entrance was regal and awe-striking, but at the same time, an unlearned and casual observer would notice the fact that after they entered walking upright, they all in unison ascended tree stumps to their respective seats and thrones in a very squirrel manner by rounding the tree stump like as if they were following a candy cane stripe or barber pole.

Without any sign of their being out of breath, each official took their seat beginning with two seats just to the right of center. These two were High Prince Tom and High Princess Margy. On the other side of center, the two seats just to the left of center, the two seats were occupied by Prince Thomas, twin brother of High Prince Tom, and Princess Margie, twin sister of High Princess Margy.

To further right of High Princess Margy sat Princess Jorie. To the left of Princess Margie sat Sir William and Madam Pearl.

Sir William and Madame Pearl, were the only two members of the council who were not also of royal blood. Yet the guidance and financial wisdom of William and Pearl, especially with their experience in negotiating with Human leaders, groups and companies was so vital that they were invited to sit on every council meeting.

High Prince Tom motioned to the assembly and to the seated council, that all should now be quiet, and reverent. When the hall was so quiet that you could hear a chipmunk's heart beating, King Tomek entered with Queen Goska.

## CASTING DOWN

Now I witnessed a wonderous sight. One that immediately brought to my mind, memories of scripture.

It began with High Prince Tom. He rose from his seat, removed his small and inauspicious crown, and laying his crown on King Tomek's lap declared, "My King and My Lord!".

Then the High Prince performed a righteous and beautiful tail-fluffing that emphasized his words, saying to King Tomek "To you I declare my honor and fealty, unchanged and unchanging".

Then High Prince Tom waited, in sublime position, until King Tomek returned High Prince Tom's crown to his head saying "you have cast your crown before me, as a sign of the day when we all will cast our crowns before the throne of the One Great God and King. Now, I return your crown to you as a sign of your leadership and authority over many, lead well."

This seen was played out for the next 6 members of the High Council, except that having no crowns, Sir William and Lady Pearl offered their signet rings of the council.

I was truly shaken by this experience.

First, each time that these great lord and lady squirrels, revered in all the land, the heroes and great leaders that always exhibited such dignity, and were the glorious subjects of all my writings, would come before the King, they did not appear as nobles, or even masters and commanders of thousands as they were. Even in their finest garments, they looked like gutter rats, so lowly and subservient to their king did they make themselves appear before him!

I just started to wonder about the words Lord and King, and Fealty and honor, and how little I understood of each word when, out of my daydreaming thoughts, I heard my name called out for the second time.

It was the voice of Queen Goska, lovely and almost musical in her speech, "Friend of the Squirrels, Emissary of the earth, approach the throne, that we might know you and be better friends."

Instant fear gripped me. I had observed that every creature presents "honors" in the assembly, such as tail-fluffing, wing flapping, or various type of mime actions, all of which had great symbolism and were synchronized to a theme that all members of their race would present that day.

I have no such honors to present in the court that I knew of.

I also was a citizen of the United States of America, of the Commonwealth of the State of Connecticut, as well as, and more importantly in my reckoning, a follower of Jesus. I have never said "Lord and King" with the passion of these animals. I thought perhaps that I could pretend that some sort of mutism disease had overcome me, and therefore my good friend Taelbaerer would speak in my name.
But what happen next was one of the most tearful reunions of my life. Marjatta and Soturi, my two squirrels, who acted as my pets on earth, until that horrid storm, the sinking of my ship, and the rescue by the Seafarer Ship, Corvina, of Saltus Fidelis, and my two squirrels having taken on their Saltus Fidelis regalia as a Lord and Lady of the Land.

It all happened so quickly. How they defended my honor and recommended me to be presented to the high council for sanctuary in Saltus Fidelis as little or long as I would choose to do so.

Then after the great ship landed, they were off! In the years that intervened, and all the adventures that took place, I never heard about them, or from them. But at this moment, they stood next to me, standing tall with a look of stern glory in their tails and on their faces.

Soturi, who was walking on my left side had placed his right paw tightly into the small of my back, with his long, shining black tail wrapped around my left leg and up over his arm and my shoulder.

v2020-02-28

((It will help to remember that the Squirrels of Saltus Fidelis, especially the Black Squirrels can achieve heights of 4.5 to 5 feet when standing)
On my right side, Marjatta had done the same from her perspective.
I suddenly found out that this tight wrapping of their arm and tails enabled them to control every muscle and ever nerve in my legs, back and shoulders like a marionette.  I found myself smoothly, almost effortlessly walking forward toward the throne of King Tomek without any will of my own, all the while with my two squirrels marching by my side, smiling sternly and lovingly.

Now we were about 10 paces from the throne.  I felt my whole body bowing gracefully, and my right arm motioning a sign of gratitude and peace.

My squirrels were also bowing gracefully.
Soturi spoke first, he began with a dutiful tail fluffing and then said,
"My King and my Lord, to you I declare my honor and fealty, unchanged and unchanging"
Marjatta repeated the same, except that she included, as all ladies did, her oath to her husband.
This all seemed to please the king very much.

Then Soturi said.  Sire, we present this day to you, Novinaja", the writer, journalist, historian, documentator (sic) and most of all, Friend of our beloved country.

v2020-02-28

King Tomek replied "You are welcome to our courts and to our country, I have read your histories and do enjoy them immensely."

I was about to answer, but then a sharp fingernail from the delicate hand of Marjatta, which was still gripping the small of my back, must have known exactly where to drill into to render a human mute. I could not move my mouth or my air passages.

While Marjatta held me mute, Soturi answered for me, "Sire, our friend Novinaja, wishes to address the court with many questions. He is ignorant of the decorum he should present before you, oh King, because in his land they have no king, and furthermore they altogether hold their leaders with a mind of derision."

Even as I was being bowed over, I could feel the gaze of each of the council members upon me. The next voice I heard was easily identifiable, it was High Princess Margy, "My King and my Lord, our good friend has shown honor to Taelbaerer and both High Prince Tom and myself. I do believe that he is sincere in his quest to rediscover our society, I am willing to vouchsafe him"

Now, it was King Tomek speaking "Arise, friend of the Squirrels".  Marjatta released her grip on my back and both Marjatta and Soturi relaxed their control over me with their tails, but still held their tails wrapped around me. This gesture brought a swift response from King Tomek, except now he started speaking in clear crisp English, "Marjatta, Soturi! From my years of consulting with humans, I know that they are unable to speak without moving their arms and hands. Release him. You are excused, or you can stay, either way, I have more than sufficient protection here.

I have spoken English to a squirrel before.  Speaking to King Tomek was truly going to be a very different experience.  "Ask us what you will." Is all that Tomek said.

I replied "King Tomek, I have known and honored many members of your council for so many years.  High Prince Tom and High Princess Margy are the greatest example of a true Lord and Lady that my mind has ever seen, but before you, their deep bow, and their words of commitment to you and lowliness when compared to you has me troubled at heart."

Now, High Prince Tom spoke up, but looking at me with a twinkle of laughter in his tail, he too responded in English, "Greatness and authority are gifts bestowed on an individual by the One Great God and HE expects each person to use these gifts to lead, to guide, to protect and reassure.  The One Great God gifts to many individuals' high power, greatness and authority, but he gifts and anoints only one to be his High King.  Next to the King, all other greatness, all power, all authority, is little more than an old garland."

Now King Tomek Spoke: "I can see that this troubles you. This is because in your culture you have no reference to the words Lord or King, which is specifically why you are here."

I was about to confirm what he had said, but King Tomek continued, "You have in your religion very odd relationships with the One Great God, and his Son, your Savior Jesus. You have one philosophy which says that The One Great God has crowned Jesus as King of your world. You call him 'Lord, this' and 'Lord, that', without any regard for the meaning of the title Lord. Your scriptures are filled with examples of reverence toward your Lord, and your minimal estate in comparison to your Lord and King. However, you have another philosophy which makes your God as familiar as a father whom you can love or argue with, and Jesus as a brother that you can second-guess or question his tactics."

I frowned.

King Tomek Continued
"You have marvelous songs such as, 'What a friend we have in Jesus', and many songs and paintings that portray our great Lord and your savior as your friend, and rightly, for he has called you so.
"But, Novinaja, I have visited your planet and received reports where the practice of this truth is that your heart is singing "What a buffoon I can be with Jesus".

v2020-02-28

You appear to think that he has bestowed on you the right of friendship so that you can forget that He is your Lord, and that you are royalty, and you can be casual with Him to the point of buffoonery or debauchery. That should never be! But it is.

Within the realms and Laws of Fantasy, and the author who has documented our existence, I receive my authority to rule from the One great God, and I am infused with a nature that cannot wax or wane, and my benevolence is purposed as a constant

Everything that you must know about the One Great God and His Son, your King, comes from your scriptures. I, Tomek, and the entire council, and the citizens of Saltus Fidelis, are about to embark with you on your journey of discovery, until you find spiritual understanding and can finally name the One Great God and his Son Jesus as Lord and King.

It is only due to your limited experience in how a Kingdom is administered, that prevents you from arriving at such an obvious conclusion as 'a King who is full of Judgement and Justice cannot be the same person as the merciful, tender-hearted King who is full of compassion.'"

Then King Tomek concluded the meeting; "I decree that I, King Tomek, Taelbaerer, and High Prince Tom, and 5 citizens from Saltus Fidelis shall meet weekly, if necessary, at a time of day to be set by Master Lord Taelbaerer on Tuesday, Thursday and Saturday with our friend and emissary from the Earth.

I entrust Taelbaerer to arrange a curriculum of study. Our friend is here to learn of Lords, Kings and Kingdoms, and we shall teach him everything, so that he may teach his people how to approach the One Great God and His Saving Son as their personal and collective Lord and King. I decree that all citizens who wish to join on this study shall sign up to share their insights beginning tomorrow

With that, King Tomek arose, silently scampered from the stadium, followed by all the council, except for Taelbaerer, who made his way back into our group.

# (MONDAY)

**OF SMALL VISION**
The next day, after my morning walk through the Rabbit Town with their beautifully manicured lawned and hedges, and perfectly aligned rows of vegetables, a symphony of sight and smells that were unlike anything that I ever encountered in person or through books on earth, I set out for a personal meeting with King Tomek.

When I woke up, there by my bedside, watching me sleep and waiting for me to wake, was the same little squirrel who had taken the liberty to bite at my toes on the previous morning.

He had a note from King Tomek, asking for me to meet him in person for a 'brief' discussion on a matter that was of particular interest to him.

"Thank you for coming, Novinaja", said King Tomek as I arrived in at our meeting place, a long grassy shoreline along one of Saltus Fidelis' inland seas. The inland seas are large bodies of water, pure and fresh, not a hint of salt or mineral content, that lay between each of the three arms of the pinwheel shape of Saltus Fidelis. Having a uniform depth, that is often referred to as the official depth of Saltus Fidelis without adding in for mountains and high valleys, of exactly 800 Kilometers, which is almost precisely the depth of the Earth's upper mantle including the continental crust, oceanic crust, asthenosphere, lithosphere.

For readers using the imperial system, 800 Kilometers is 2,624,800 feet or 497 Miles.

v2020-02-28

"Novinaja, I have spent much of life as an emissary of science, technology and the arts to the presidents and prime ministers of your nations. Although, by international code, no person from Saltus Fidelis would receive credit or be named, we were present as members of science and safety at the intergovernmental meeting of UNESCO in Paris in December 1951, when it established **C**onseil **E**uropéen pour la **R**echerche **N**ucléaire. (CERN)

King Tomek: "We supported the project with funds in 1993, and advised new safeguards after the incident of 2008. But for all the research and science of your planet, the one postulate that they will not understand is that their field of view is too small.

King Tomek: "Here is my Bottom Line:
Taelbaerer is convinced that the system of "Civil Disobedience" will keep all men from yielding to any appreciation of the words "Lord" or "King" and by extent, will keep them always distant from their own Lord and King.
I am also convinced that what stands between all men and their understanding and desire for their Lord and King is their narrow Vision, and man's reckless desire to put God into a box of their own understanding.

King Tomek: "Simply, what is blinding them is their narrow vision. They cannot see God, they cannot feel him, or touch him, and others have ignorantly hurled challenges toward clouds or sunbeams, limiting their beliefs to a God that lives in the Physical worlds.

v2020-02-28

King Tomek: "I contended with an astronomer of your Earth who had insisted that there is no God, because he had catalogued every star and has still never seen God, that his field of vision was too small.  So together we accessed the Hubble Space telescope library and magnified images into far distances. I still argued that his field of vision was too small.


King Tomek: "Next, he presented me a recording from Voyager 1, which had left the Solar System in the summer of 2012, but still sent back one more transmission in the spring of 2013.
I said, your field of vision is still too small.

We visited Berkerly, California and the $27 million electron microscope. Currently the most powerful designed and able to make images to a resolution of half the width of a hydrogen atom

King Tomek: "I was impressed, yet not impressed, and I explained to him as much.  Your world vision is still too small. Finally, I had someone annoyed enough to ask me "how so""

King Tomek: " "How does your scope of vision explain imagination, inspiration, meta-physics? How does your scope of vision explain that you are talking to me?
I Have seen your own artists imagine and depict in movies, amazing details of materials thousands of times smaller than what you just showed me! I have seen your artists imagine and demonstrate entire civilizations that have lived and died out among the stars in less than three generations of your Earth's years.

I have seen and listened to artist and musicians inspired to create poetry and music that touches a person's soul. I believe in the Soul, I have seen it, felt it, experienced it.

Finally King Tomek paused from his speech. I had to chuckle inside for just a moment thinking "wow, these squirrels are certainly long-winded".

So, I replied to King Tomek. "I think that I understand what you want me to learn is this:

First, No matter how hard I look using reason, physics or science, I cannot prove or disprove God.
Second, God inhabits ALL the realms of existences, the physical, and every thought, every imagination, every inch of our soul.

King Tomek stopped me flat.
"You stupid man. Did I ever say that? God does NOT INHABIT. God is Sovereign over, God is Better than, God is More than, God is Beyond that. He is not some fairy-tale energy, force or field. Now try it again!

"My Lord and King, Tomek, I give you honor, and beg your forbearance.", I started out.
"That's a better start!", replied King Tomek.

I continued on,

"First, No matter how much I use reason, physics or science, others may or may not choose to understand or may even ridicule the obvious evidences of God."
"Next, As for myself, I know that God is sovereign over all of physics, He is better than every thought and every imagination, and He is more than the eternal soul."
Then I paused for moment, and said, "My Lord and my King Tomek, just in reciting that line, I have overcome so much of what has been holding me back. I am so grateful. I am ready to move on!

v2020-02-28

## (TUESDAY)

**OF LORDS**

The next morning, I hastened over to Taelbaerer's, I made a point to be at least 10 minutes early, but alas, I was the last to arrive. As soon as I walked in, King Tomek stood up, presented a brief but regal tail fluffing, and sat down. Then High Prince Tom, Princess Jorie, Taelbaerer, High Herald Pinita and Red Acorn Scientist Nufter all performed their best tail fluffing.

King Tomek then turned to me and commanded, "it is inappropriate, given our mission and purpose that you, our friend, do not come each morning with your own court greetings. Please tell us what art, song or dance you would like to demonstrate before our group each day before we begin our studies.

Fortunately, I had already thought about this the night before, so my answer was quick and clear, "Sire, King of Saltus Fidelis, in the manner and customs of my peoples, I should offer the convocation prayer to the One Great God and his Son. I will do so in the High Furorem tongue of the squirrels and in English.

Although King Tomek's face was stern and without reaction, his tail was giggling with delight as he said "Yes, Indeed, our friend, we shall like that very much".

I presented the following prayer in High Furorem and in English.

## 62

Dominus, Deus caeli,
Deus magnus et terribilis est:
qui custodis pactum et dilectione
diligentibus se
et custodientibus mandata tua:
sit auris tua attendens
aperi oculos tuos, et audire
orationem quam servus tuus orat coram te,
da nobis sapientia

LORD, the God of heaven,
the great and awesome God,
who keeps his covenant of love
with those who love him
and keep his commandments
let your ear be attentive
and your eyes open to hear
the prayer your servant is praying before you
Grant us wisdom


When I was finished, Taelbaerer's tail twinkled a little as he leaned over and whispered to me, "My great grandfather, Taelbaerer of the East was a good friend of Nehemiah."

Then King Tomek began. " I shall begin with a simple postulate. That whenever any group of individuals gather for any endeavor, whether it be to build a bridge or a nation, the first order of business is to choose, or acquiesce to a leader for that group or endeavor. "

"Then, I shall add two corollaries," added Princess Jorie, "First, That the size of the group does not matter, it can be as few as three, or as great as thousands, and second, that the desire to have a leader outweighs the task, or the urgency of the task, for both will fail without the leader."

"I also have two corollaries", added High Prince Tom, "that since most of the participants of a group do not wish to hold Leadership, the selection of leadership is limited to personality types that tend to self-aggrandizement.

After recovering from the shock of what the high Prince said, I spoke up, "My observation is this, histories are always written by the strong and by the victors, and second, those who write histories tend to portray the leaders of their enemies as barbarians and Idiots.

King Tomek replied "I agree, and you all see, we have much to discuss. Now, let me pose to you, what is the worst challenge facing all realms and peoples and individuals today?

There was light discussion for about 30 minutes, and finally the Nufter, speaking for the conclusion arrived at by the group said
# "ANGER"

Then, to heighten the point, I replied "This is no more evident than in the Human world, whenever I am home on back on Earth, there is concern for Global Warming, Political division, disease, depression and more."

I paused, since I was actually ashamed to be so honest in front of these squirrels, but finally I continued "there is complete ignorance of the single most destructive wave overtaking our planet, the crescendo of Anger."

"Everyone is Angry, and they are angry all the time at everything! I began to shout. "Anger seethes on the highways and in the ballparks, it is a catalyst of political and religious systems and is found in the youngest child and the oldest adult! It kills motorists, and divides families! It causes children to murder each other!"

"Peace, my friend," interrupted Tomek, "I can see how Anger is stirred up in you at the very mention of Anger.

"In Saltus Fidelis", explained Jodie, "it is our law that no resident is permitted to be angry with another individual. The law states that all anger can only be directed toward a particular incident, or particular instrument, but not at the individuals involved in the incident, or the instruments that they wielded.

Therefore, our ire was not directed at Corvis Tuus, that he killed Peggy, rather our outrage was directed at the long period of détente and mistrust between our nations that led up to that horrible day, and we discovered that both we, and them, were determined to end these misunderstandings.

High Prince Tom added:
"Saltus Fidelis courts will not hear proceedings against a citizen or alien for just being who they are. It is all about intentions and actions that leads to damage or injury. In such cases, the results of the damages would be considered when determining to what degree that the individual or individuals will be prevented from causing them again, and protecting society from a repeat of their actions.

I asked "To what degree will you prevent them?"

High Prince Tom replied "A heinous crime deserves dreadful prevention."

King Tomek decided it was time to get our conversation back on track to the discussion that we had assembled for:

"Let us talk of Lords", Said Tomek

"Yes!" I agreed, "the only Lord that I know is my Lord Jesus, and yet, although I call him my Lord, I wish that I understood my own words."

"Understanding your own words is certainly wise, too many fools use their words carelessly", observed Taelbaerer.

King Tomek then began with his basic instruction:
"Let us begin with the basic knowledge of your own Earth. Your own dictionary describes Lord as "one having power and authority over others: a ruler by hereditary right or preeminence to whom service and obedience are due"
This definition has both merits and failing. It is incomplete in that it stresses the negatives, and presupposes a climate where civil disobedience can thrive, and anger may take deep roots.

"The Lord Jesus is a perfect example of a Lord, and one that every Lord and Lady of Saltus Fidelis seeks to emulate.

"The Lord Jesus was anointed and appointed by the King, after evidencing himself worthy of rule and authority by his own service, compassion and sacrifice."

Now High Prince Tom spoke:
"Although few approach me as, "Lord High Prince Tom", it is due to a personal choice that I made long ago when I was a young squirrel. But it is very true, that below the king, I am the Highest Lord in the land.
I am certain that a Lord who claims hereditary right or preeminence to wield the title, must have proven his worthiness to become a Lord through a quest that will demonstrate his compassion, service and sacrifice. In all the lands of Fantasy and most certainly in Saltus Fidelis, even a lord born by birth may not be given their title, unless he or she has been shown to be rightful and genuine through quest and sacrifice. Novinaja, your twisted view of evil kingdoms must certainly have come from kingdoms where Lords and Ladies took their titles without quest or sacrifice, and know little of hardship or compassion.

"Another lesson that I learned from your Lord, the Lord, Jesus" continued High Prince Tom, " is that a Lord who claims birthright must first honor his King at all times. Even if the Lord is a King, then he must honor the High King.

High Princess Margy had been asked to share about a Lord's duty as judge and magistrate. High Princess Margy resides on almost 75% of all court proceedings of Saltus Fidelis, and 100% of those that involved foreign entities.

"A Lord or Lady must take on the heart of nobility." She began, "Since only princes and princesses are permitted to be lawyers, We have created a list of four ethics that all who decide legal matters live by:
First, because we are all Lords and Ladies, we shall never allow vainglory to persuade us.
Second, since wealth is of little use to us, we always have what we need at our disposal, no bribe can entice us.
Third, since we have studied many years under the great Taelbaerers, no clever speech can confound us.
And Last, we may take office in the courts only after we are married, so that no beauty can sway us.

All this time, I was feverishly taking notes and writing down all that was said, all the while thinking about how the Lords and Ladies of Saltus Fidelis patterned every aspect of their life around the Lord Jesus, when he walked on the Earth.

Since all agreed that I received a wealth of instruction for this day we all went to our homes to rest and contemplate.

## (Wednesday)

The next day we were not scheduled for an actual meeting, so I decided to get up early and take a brisk walk toward the shining mountains in the distance. The sun that we now shared with Earth was somewhat of an enigma to those living on Saltus Fidelis and the inhabitants of Earth. As I might have mentioned too many times before, as old men are wont to do, the worlds of Physics, such as your Earth, Sun, stars, etc., are usually not affected or impacted by the worlds of Fantasy.
However, in contrast, the worlds of Fantasy are very often affected by the events of physical worlds around them. They do feel the passing shadow of the Earth blocking the Sun, and they feel the warmth of our sun itself.

Sorry, back to the story, since the joining of Saltus Fidelis and Earth, the disk of Saltus Fidelis which spins on a wild and wriggly line all over the globe, is of such size and mass that it should cast a great shadow on the Earth every day, but since it is Fantasy, it does not. However, a cool physical shadow will often be cast on Saltus Fidelis as it spins around this earth.

v2020-02-28

This was one of the mornings, it was generally a warm day, but the shadow of Earth was predicted to be persistent for most of the day.  It was perfect for a little walking, a little jogging, a little stretching.

Very shortly after I started on my way, alongside me, I thought most uncharacteristic for his age and status, Taelbaerer came bounding up beside me.

I thought I could outrace him, and best him at something, but then I realized that he was a squirrel, and running on all fours gave him quite an advantage.  About 10 minutes ahead of me, he was sitting on a stump, gnawing on a stack of Acorns.

"Can I talk to you some more, Taelbaerer, while we walk?"
"Certainly, Novinaja, should I walk slowly, or talk slowly, so you can keep up?", with that, his tail shook with laughter.

"Taelbaerer," I blurted out "I understand so much more about my Lord, seeing that in order to become worthy of the title 'Lord' he had to pass so many tests!"

 "Where did you get that theology?  Remember that your Lord was always God and Lord, it was not an earned right.  Nevertheless, two things happened, all of Saltus Fidelis has learned the lessons of how to become Lords and Ladies, and all of Saltus Fidelis has learned how to love Lords and Ladies"

v2020-02-28

ME: "I don't understand your second part, how do your citizens learn to love without question and blind obedience?"

Taelbaerer: "That is the lesson that you should have learned from your Lord Jesus. Certainly, he did not need to perform any of his deeds to declare his lordship over the earth. All things were created through Him, and apart from Him, nothing that has being, was created. He was offered complete Lordship for the parlor trick of kneeling to a demon, and refused. No, He performed his acts of Lordship to give you and your world, the everlasting GIFT that He could be trusted!

"It is the same reason that our Lords and Ladies must perform their sacrifices. To prove that they can be trusted."

Me: "So you are saying that trust is the cause of obedience?

Taelbaerer: It is one of them, and it is a very good one.
There are all the matters that we have discussed, the need for a leader, that civil obedience is the better state of man, not civil disobedience, since love and compassion flow from the throne and back to it.

I decided to keep pushing "What is Fealty?"

Taelbaerer: It is a pledge to your Lord that you give more than your trust and love. Trust and love are saying that you have given your heart. Fealty is saying that you are ready to give the rest of yourself, your strength (sword), your honor (ego), and your will (all your physical abilities) at the beck and call of your lord. In Saltus Fidelis it is an optional oath, but a sincere oath, that when the Lord has need of you, you are there.

Me: "Taelbaerer, I can understand that answer. There are still many things that bother me. In all of history, it seems to me that nations that are built on a monarchy, such as Saltus Fidelis, are open to tyranny, oppression, and domination of the unfortunate."

I feared that I may have offended Taelbaerer, but there was no appearance of offence in his tail or face, so I continued, "Furthermore, do not monarchies of the past and current depend on coercion and control of the subjected masses, placing them into assigned castes with rewards and punishments to keep them in their place?"

I pressed on, with Taelbaerer deeply focusing on my words,

"In my society's past, we broke free of such a tyrannical monarchy and set up safeguards in our constitutions to prevent a monarchy from ever being established within our boarders. Every American child knows that absolute power corrupts absolutely, and the end of any monarchy can only be evil.

v2020-02-28

I continued on
"Now please understand me, with much bloodshed, our nation was born out of a Monarchy, yet all of my days as of follower of Jesus, all my songs and prayers are to return to a monarchy. A monarchy of God, and Jesus as King. Taelbaerer, here in Saltus Fidelis you seem to have discovered how to have a good monarchy. Since that is the end of all men, excuse me, all creatures, I must, no, I can go no further without putting the One Great God, as you say, and His Son, as both Lord and King in my Life."

Without sign of being offended, Taelbaerer replied,
"Finally, my dear friend, you have revealed the truth of your suspicions. For that, know that I and the whole council will love and trust you all the more.
Now, as to your statements: All of your statements might be true in a society where Civil Disobedience was the law of the land, but in a land that had not learned civil disobedience, the King would not disobey his duties before God to love and govern, and the people would respond with love.

"In Saltus Fidelis, the Kingdom is simplified. Regarding our religion, we are unfaltering, almost as you would say one-dimensional. We are ruled by the laws of our Lord. The moral, social and worship laws of Saltus Fidelis demonstrate the One Great God as our Highest King, and His Son as our King and our first Lord.

v2020-02-28

Next, we have our king, our ruler, Tomek. Tomek derives all of his authority only by divine anointing of the One Great God. As there is no need for sacrifice, we do not have priests as in your culture, but, in your thoughts, you might consider Tomek as the King and Priest before God. Next are the Lordly Princes and Princesses, then the Lords and Ladies, then those squirrels of high honor, then all the citizens."

"As to your next question, why do citizens love, even unto death?
For most squirrels of our land, because of unbroken faith in their king, it is each individual's personal oath of fealty that causes one to regard even their own life as a precious gift to give to their Lord, but give it they will when required. For these, and for others, if one is willing to give up your precious life to serve your lord, how much more pleasure it is to still be breathing and be able to serve your lord."

We all exist. We are born, we have an existence, and we pass on to the mercy of the One Great God and His Son Jesus.
We all exist, that is the fact. The GIFT, is that we are each called to live well. From the most athletic to the most infirmed, living beyond existing is the desire of every creature. Is that not the words of your sacred document: Life, Liberty and Pursuit of Happiness?

To live well is to have a cause or a reason.
To have a cause or a reason with a leader that supports, guides and honors you as you "live well" is a great blessing.
Aligning yourself to your leader, and his company will provide you great companionship, peace and joy.
If the opportunities to further the mutual causes and reasons that you hold dear require personal danger or death, you will want a leader who carefully plans that you and your comrades will survive.

Novinaja, it has been decades since there has been a collective reason or cause for individuals in your country to die for. And yet men and women continue to give their fealty to the Flag of your country and the freedom and justice that it stands for. A truly noble act since they offer their life to the dream, the past, the present, and the future of your nation.

So do not act surprised that every creature on Saltus Fidelis offers their fealty to the King and Queen. If you want examples of personal fealty in action, you can ask the 2.1 million men and women who have sworn personal fealty in your own country.

I replied "Taelbaerer, you have spoken very well. I never thought of our Armed Forces in that manner. Two million or more individuals all swearing fealty to our flag and the nation that it represents. I do not question the fealty of your own citizens!"

Then opening a large picture book, he began slowly paging through years of news-clippings, allowing me to remember with horror, the intensity of Anger in the 1960's and 1970's, as it romped through cities like a monstrous Godzilla, burning neighborhoods to the ground. And in the remainder of the 20$^{th}$ century as Anger went underground, infiltrating society into sniper shootings, school shooters, aggressive drivers, and violence.

All the while, as Hate and Anger intensified, it kept us from seeing what it was doing to us: Me First, All About Me, I matter more than a million others. If you are not the same as me, then you are a hater."

And that was the surface. The Government was hastily trying to level all layers of society, or at least bring down the middle class into the same quality of life that they would raise up the poverty class to..

Taelbaerer then said "In your country, you have created a caste system based on wealth and pride, there exists a 'forgotten class' of uncounted children in trafficking and homeless vagabonds, a lower class, middle class, completely indebted middle class and an upper class. At least 81% of your society is completely in debt to a bank or finance agency and are less secure than the poverty class that they think themselves superior of."

ME: "Please stop! It is true, underneath the crust of what seems normal living for so many people, lies layers of seething magna of the uncounted and the uncountable, who I, like so many others find easy to ignore while we go on our normal lives." Then Taelbaerer took his great furry tail and gently rubbed my head and back and slowly soothed out the thoughts and horrors that my mind just envisioned. After a while, I felt as though I could talk again.

But it Taelbaerer who spoke first: "Look, it is evening, and we have arrived back at your home, please rest and think about all we discussed. Tomorrow, our session will convene again."

# (THURSDAY)

The Next Evening, after a day of study and much thought and prayer, it was time for my next session with the outstanding group of royalty from this land. I remember reading how Gulliver was invited by the king of the Lilliputians to be the guest of the land, but I felt my experience was profoundly different from Gulliver's. I was gaining deep admiration for the court of Saltus Fidelis, overlooking the fact that they were mere squirrels, because their words, their civilization and deeds demonstrated a poised and reverent society that had perfect order without fear of rule, but rather with love of rulers.

As I was heading up to my meeting this evening, I was not interacting with mere squirrels, I was interacting with a great and intelligent alien race, whose form did not matter, and I was representing, or doing my best to represent, the very best of mankind.

This second meeting was held in the great library of Saltus Fidelis, created by constructing large edifices around several close growing trees, creating as single huge building. The entrances of the building were accessed through any one of five large trees, and climbing internally to the third height (about 40 feet), where the complete structure was laid out. All of the staircases were designed for the average squirrel height of about 4-4 1/2 feet tall, except for the great White Oak tree which was entrance number four. There, the grand staircase was designed to accommodate visitors as tall as 7 feet, which suited me just fine.

v2020-02-28

When I arrived, Mr. William and Mrs. Pearl were waiting for me. These were two highly honored squirrels, and also part of the court of seven. They escorted me up the Great White Oak Staircase to our meeting room where King Tomek, High Prince Tom and High Princess Margy and Taelbaerer were already waiting.

King Tomek opened the proceedings: Let us begin with our customary giving of honors. At which each of the 6 High Court squirrels demonstrated a beautiful tail fluffing, and at the end, I recited my prayer, as I did the time before.
King Tomek then asked me "Novinaja, our beloved Taelbaerer tells us the tale of your visit and your walk with him yesterday. I earnestly desire to know your conclusions from your own soul" I was prepared for this, and actually eager to talk about it, so I began: "King Tomek, beloved King of Saltus Fidelis, compassionate ruler and first emissary to my own Country where your invisible advice is a help to our leaders, God Bless you! I cannot offer my fealty, although I wish that I could, but I have already promised it to my nation and government, and repeated it often in a national pledge. I do offer you my obedience in all respects, my honor and my love, and I do this from all sincerity of mind and heart.

King Tomek smiled his appreciation, and said "I thank you for that, but that did not answer my question.

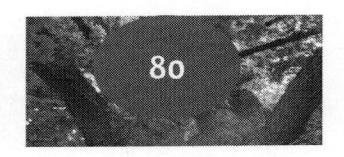

Slightly discouraged by his response, I went on, "When I first arrived, I harbored a sense of cynical wonderment at all that I saw, as if it was too good, too. I felt that all the citizens, even the Lords and Ladies were pretending, acting as it were, in order to somehow impress me. But as I continued to spend time, I discovered that most often no one noticed that I was around, and yet a peace that I could not understand seemed to fill the hearts of every creature of Saltus Fidelis.

"It was not until our talks, that I was exposed to how thoroughly conditioned I had become to believe that civil disobedience, not civil obedience could and should be the norm of all creatures.

I could see that everyone was closely listening to me, so I continued,
"So deep had the notion of Civil Disobedience been ingrained into me as necessary for freedom, from Biblical stories of heroes casting off the bonds of their captors, to the American Revolution, to the intellectual revolution in college campuses every year, that I could not accept any alternative. But you, my dear squirrel friends have shown me what can be, what must be and what will be.
I believed that "I" was always number 1, My own leader, in charge of my own fate, through hard work, I was self-determinate. Now I understand that too is a fairy-tale, the worst lies of fiction. I survive and thrive when working together with others under the clear guidance of a good leader. I now see the true position of a leader; the value of a leader and how civil obedience works best in small groups as it must in larger groups.

I continued:
"Most of all, I understand, my Lord, the wonderment of any individual who seeks by skill or honor, or is thrust into by birthright, the position of Lord or Lady. The compassion, sacrifices, and dedication that is given to those who are to lead is unimaginable in my country."

This unimaginable character of a Lord is what I have been missing in my life when I say my Lord Jesus. He is the one to who I give my whole fealty, He is the one who has proven over and over that HE alone is worthy to lead and to be followed, and that I can follow Him without reservation, without hiding civil disobedience in my heart for lack of trust.

King Tomek replied "Great words of the mind may take time to become overwhelming purposes of life, my friend. Nevertheless, our meeting scribes have written everything that you just said, so that you can read it, remember and purpose it to your heart.

I was standing during my entire dissertation, and now I took my seat as we continued our meeting.

## OF COMMONERS AND KINGS
We had just begun our meeting, and I started by summarizing my story about my new understanding of the expression 'Lord' whenever I pray 'Lord Jesus,'; when Taelbaerer leaned forward, wrapping his long and bushy tail around him like a warm cardigan and began:

"My King and my Lord Tomek, you are wise and compassionate, however we must not hasten to build the pride of completion in the heart of Novinaja, lest he feels that he has no need of more knowledge."

Then, turning toward me, he continued,

"Novinaja, you have learned some, but you have so much to learn. Yes, you recognize that in your own heart that you feel as an outsider looking in. You have made strides in appreciating that you are a confessed follower of the son of the One Great God. Your own writings and books attest that you are now in every way, except figuratively, are made to be a son of God. You have become Royalty!

All of your reading and learning is bound up in your neck!"*

He paused and looked closely at me.

As Taelbaerer continued, I began to feel that I, on behalf of humanity, was again under interrogation


(*head knowledge, not heart knowledge)

v2020-02-28

"And I am proven by your expressionless face that I am correct! The fact that You Are Royalty does not seem to weigh heavily on your mind and heart like it does for all the royalty of Saltus Fidelis. If fact, I dare say, the fact that you are royalty barely matters to you at all! You are royalty, preferring to live as a mere commoner! You are now part of God's 'system', but you'd rather stay comfortable in the system that you have been in.
Being a follower of Jesus, it seems, does not require much from you, because you have been void of the concept of 'Lord', but being Royalty, that's where you will have to make too many changes.
You don't want to be royalty, you are happy being a commoner, thereby you can still question his system, or those in his system. Is any part of what I am saying untrue?

Obviously, Taelbaerer had completely changed the mood in the room, but no one else spoke to come to my aide, everyone was hush, waiting for my reply. I was seated, elbows on my knees, my face buried in my hands, half enraged, half crying. The bottom line, huge layers of my inner protective 'pharisee' were being exposed and uncharitably ripped away by this furry beast. I sat and contemplated for what seemed like an hour.

With my hands again in my face, (a posture a found myself taking too often) I began with a sneer in my voice.
"How is it that in an instant of time we have gone from classroom to courtroom? I will answer you when you answer me."

v2020-02-28

"Our Dearest Novinaja, Friend, you are not on trial, these questions are not meant to insult, they are meant to refine you like a refiner's fire, we need to burn off everything that you must unlearn so that you have the ability to learn. We love you, our Friend. There is not one question, not one statement, that Taelbaerer has spoken, that he, High Prince Tom and I did not anguish over for many hours." The voice, of course was lovely, soothing and came from High Princess Margy.

I lowered my hand and opened my eyes.
I mumbled to myself, but loud enough to confess to those around me, "How many times that I have read, sung, and prayed, 'I am a child of God', and yet not once did those words ever sink so deep as to change the way that I behaved or lived. I always read and sung and prayed those words as a reminder to God, that he was responsible to take care of me.

So, you are correct in every way. I never considered that I was made royalty, you are correct that I enjoyed playing the pitiful commoner, always floundering, always in that state of civil disobedience, which in our religious culture we name as sin, but then argue about the severity of it.

I continued, "I now make my pledge before all present in this court, that I shall not refer to myself or others as being a 'child of God' without believing that this means that I, that we, are Royalty, and being Royalty, we do not act like commoners. We are above such nonsense; we are special and set apart.

"Again, you have spoken well", said Tomek with an air of calm delight in his voice, "This is the message that you must bring home to your people, to stop living as commoners, if they are to claim to be children of God, then behave as the royalty that they have become, and stop using the phrase merely to conjure up the divine protection of the one Great God or merely as an incantation to insure His provisions"

Now Taelbaerer began, "Dear friend, Novinaja, before King Tomek and the court determined to have these sessions with you, which has been for your learning and for all your people through your writings, we came to a conclusion, which we hope is agreeable to you. Our discussion about a King would be restricted to the relationship a King has to his citizenry who love his rule, who are committed to the principles, merits, rewards and bounty of civil obedience. We will leave out discussions of the dealings of a King where civil disobedience is encountered. Is this agreeable to you?"

I was actually very sad. It would be an incomplete report. I replied "Could we discuss the two separately? I rather not leave out the harsh king and only have the loving king, since in my own scripture, it seems that my Old Testament is filled with pages of a harsh and punishing King, while the New Testament is filled with pages of a loving, healing and forgiving King."

High Prince Tom suddenly had a very worried look come over his tail and over his brow.  Cautiously he began "Novinaja, we, I, well, there is a great deal of Biblical misunderstanding that you possess. I believed that you were well versed in the scriptures. Maybe you have a slightly better than cursory understanding?

Now it was my turn to be confused, "what do you mean, my lord, High Prince?"

"Simply this," continued High Prince Tom "The One True God presented himself so lovingly in both your 'Testaments', and his Son Jesus presented Himself as both loving and caring and stern and judgmental.  Wrath is an immediate response to all forms of civil disobedience and love and caring is an immediate response to those who have the character of civil obedience.

"Did not Nehemiah your prophet of old say of the One Great God: 'LORD, the God of heaven, the great and awesome God, who keeps his covenant of love with those who love him and keep civil obedience in their hearts.*", Continued prince Tom
* and keep his commandments,

"And didn't the One Great God also say of himself 'The LORD, the LORD, the compassionate and gracious God, slow to anger, abounding in love and faithfulness, maintaining love to thousands, and forgiving even civil disobedience. * ",  Added King Tomek
*wickedness, rebellion and sin.

v2020-02-28

Finally Taelbaerer added, "But the One Great God is not a Fool, he is not a wishing well or a puppet. For He also says of Himself. 'Yet he does not leave the civil disobedient * unpunished; he punishes the children and their children for the sin of the parents to the third and fourth generation."
*Guilty

"And Jesus, the Lord that you follow, warned you this ""Then he will say to those on his left, **'Depart from me, you who are cursed, into the eternal fire prepared for the devil and his angels"**, and to whom was he referring to? Those followers engaged in civil disobedience through *willful inaction* and blind inattentiveness."

I shuddered to think of the number of times that I engaged in this very type of civil disobedience.

"So," said Taelbaerer, "Can you understand, and agree to the possibility that a society of civil obedience is not the same as a society of oppressed, subjugated, controlled or dominated peoples?

"Yes, I see that civil disobedience does not have to be the natural state of society, and a society that has learned civil obedience to their King and the One Great God has contentment with great gain.", I replied

"Do you understand that a King can both rule and love his nation where the heart of civil obedience rules?" asked Taelbaerer

"Yes, I see that in your beloved King Tomek, Lord of Saltus Fidelis"

v2020-02-28

"Very well," concluded Tomek, "we shall talk of Kings.

"A King is greater than a Lord, that is the first principle that you must know. A King is always a Lord, but there are many Lords in a Kingdom who are servants of the King"

King Tomek continued:
"A King may only receive his right to the throne through the power and manipulation of time and events by the One Great God. A King might also receive his title to the throne through birthright or conquest of the throne's prior occupant. Therefor, you see that your Lord Jesus, conquered SIN and DEATH and took his throne as your King in heaven and on earth.

"In Saltus Fidelis, we have a theology of the trinity. We know it exists, we believe it, but the explanations are so elusive we do not try.

"Therefore, laying aside all theological ideals for the sake of storytelling, we describe the One Great God as the HIGH KING of everything past, present and is to come, Jesus as the King of Heaven and all creation, and the Spirit as the Highest Lord Emissary to every soul. This explanation works well for all the worlds of Fantasy known to Saltus Fidelis.

"years ago, it was brought to my attention that you attempted to discover my lineage, or at least, my age. I earnestly read your books to uncover what you concluded, only to find that you discovered nothing from all your research.

Tomek Continued:

"The truth is, all the inhabitants of Saltus Fidelis live exceptionally long lives, such as recorded of your earth before your millennial flood. We are killed in wars, but somehow, we do not seem to age. In that manner, we are much like the high elves that C.S. Lewis wrote about in his travels.

"How I came about, or who my parents are, I do not remember. There are volumes of books and scrolls in Taelbaerer's special vault that only a Goodly Fox, the 'angelic-like' creatures that you have written about in other books, are allowed to read, and in them are the stories of my birth and more.

"You already know the wonderful story of how Queen Goska, the lovely Maiden Queen, came to be, for you have written so much about her in your first book, and your book has become required reading in all our schools.

Tomek continued: "You know how often the Queen and I are away, emissaries ourselves to the nations of Earth, instructing them in the ways of Saltus Fidelis, and setting up fair trade acts between the physical universe and the universe of Fantasy. "Why do you think that we are able to do this?"

"Is it because High Prince Tom and High Princess Margy are so capable rulers?", I asked.

v2020-02-28

"No! said Tomek, "to suggest that they could be as good as a ruler as I, their king, would be High Treason. To discover that this was a desire hidden in their hearts would bring swift sentence upon them, and anyone who conspired with them. No, regardless of how well they serve in the ministries of their offices as High Prince and High Princess, or even the whole court; regardless of their victories and love that they have procured for the crown at home, they are not great rulers in my stead. "

Tomek's voice was becoming far more 'kingly' for lack of a better description,
"They are not replacements; nor are they place holders for my rule. So Again, why do we leave them to lead and rule our people while we are away, and why do the High Prince, High Princess, and all the princess and princesses agree to perform their duties so diligently?"

I sat with a blank stare, not sure, exactly what answer Tomek wanted from me, then I heard myself saying, the word "Is it for trust?"

"Trust!" affirmed Tomek
"Trust!", gleefully repeated all else in the room.
"Their trust is given to me in their oath of obedience and fealty. We make our covenant of trust which insures the continual operations of our land. In trusting that I, as King, will support, either by edict, or by treaties with other worlds, all that my council does, I am able to trust the council and my royal court to dispense the goodness and laws of Saltus Fidelis exactly as if I was there.

"Trust is like a great bridge held up by huge cables, securing long spans between persons. The breaking of trust is like the cutting of cables, and collapsing of the bridge. Letters of love and forgiveness may pour across the chasm through any sort of technological means, but to rebuild that bridge, to regain and support the overwhelming weight of trust, the repairs and redesign of the structure may take a good part of a lifetime.

Tomek concluded:
"The moral of the story, Saltus Fidelis lives on trust. So many other worlds have died away because of the lack of it. Your own world is in great jeopardy today. "

Then Madame Pearl, who was part of today's group spoke up. "It is true that our Lord and King, Tomek must be able to trust us, but if you have been observant around the Kingdom, you will noticed that every citizen, from the most Noble Squirrel, to the millions of quiet and industrious rabbits have a sincere and complete trust in their King, and His appointed court.

"Trust in our leadership has become almost a byline for a joke in my society,", I sadly replied, "but judging by the controlling laws and taxes that our leadership continuously writes for and against the populace, it appears that even the leaders have no trust for us, the citizens that they lead.

v2020-02-28

"Yes", said Madame Pearl, "I am somewhat of a history lover of your American history of the last 100 years. There is a celebrated document in your country, called your Declaration of Independence. I am certain you have heard of it, although, if you are an average citizen of your nation you have never fully read it. There is one sentence of the document which is mutated itself into the very genetics of every man, woman and child of your country. Taken out of context, at worst it is a call to anarchy and at best it is a celebration that pins medals on the chests of heroes of civil disobedience. The line reads "That whenever any Form of Government becomes destructive of these ends, it is the Right of the People to alter or to abolish it"
"But,", I retorted, "I do not think that many of those who read it are on the fringe of violence and crime"

"**Civil Disobedience**" interrupted Taelbaerer.

I continued "Ok, for the sake of our discussions, civil disobedience, actually know of those words, or are acting upon the decree of those words."

Madame Pearl continued: "Since the 1960s your colleges have taught this theme. The Term "Question Authority" attributed to Timothy Leary, but has actually existed in the Human DNA since Socrates, was Popularized in the late 1960s with frustrations of the prolonged war, presidential recall, 'Tune Out Drop Out' and more. Today in your pseudointellectual colleges, youth are taught not to make the world better, but to change it.

I finally decided to ask the obvious question.
"Isn't it possible to live as responsible citizen of my country, espousing the good of civil disobedience, and also to live as a responsible citizen, being a follower of Jesus, but espousing a life of civil obedience?

Soon, even I could see the silliness of the question.

I sat silently for quite a while.

Then I asked. " Is there any more teaching that you wish to give me at this time about a king?"

Taelbaerer, who had been the moderator of the group since we started, then declared "We can all see that you are burdened with todays discussion, and that you need to resolve things in your mind. By your leave, my Lord and King, Tomek, I counsel that We should conclude now and meet again the night after tomorrow.

King Tomek motioned for all to be seated. He stood, and asked for me to give my invocation to close our group. Then he said "Peace to all. Know the One Great God".

v2020-02-28

## (FRIDAY)
The next Morning, I was sharply woken up before dawn by the noisy sound of excited young squirrels rapping at my door and throwing acorn husks at my window to stir me.
"Wake Up! Wake Up! Or you'll miss them."

Sleepily, I barely yawned the question, "miss what?"

We are approaching a wonderful set of 'Ural Hops' taking place on the peanut arm.!
 It is rolling directly over the Appalachians from south to north all day and everyone is going there for the rides.

In the prior books, I explain in greater detail what the Ural Hops are, but to summarize: They are named for an experience attained when an arm of Saltus Fidelis rides along the surface of the Earth so as to be affected by the contours of the surface. This creates an entirely unstable undulating motion to the ground beneath your feet which can rise or fall hundreds or thousands of feet like huge waves as one of the arms of Saltus Fidelis essentially drapes itself over the Earth.

Of course, since the world of Physics is not impacted by the world of Fantasy, no one on our planet knows of this occurring. Extremely imaginative people may sense a warm glow inside or feel a sudden wind where there is none.

But on Saltus Fidelis the story is completely different, and my young squirrel friends were determined to have me join them this time. The favorite game of all creatures, be they Squirrel, rabbit, possum, chipmunk or any of thousands of other species, is to wait until the land "crowns" beneath them. Then everyone runs and jumps as high and far as they can and hopes to land on the next crowning land. Of course, many fall short and land on soil softened to the texture of marshmallows from the undulations. So, everyone has fun, and rarely does anyone get hurt, except clutzy old me.

My first 2 jumps were spectacular, I actually made it from the crest of one large hill to the next, as Saltus Fidelis moved rapidly northward over the Appalachians, but on my 3rd attempt, for whatever silly notion, I crossed my ankles, missed the hill and fell into the soft soil below, with 2 badly sprained ankles.

If you never tried the Ural Hops, you must go to Saltus Fidelis and have a go at it. It is like hang gliding, base jumping and suspended animation all at once.

Anyways, I was already limping home from the Ural Hops, and it was still before noon, when Taelbaerer caught up to me.

"Enjoying yourself?" He asked.
"Yes, all fun and games until someone loses a leg", I joked
"nah, you'll be fine,

"Novinaja," Taelbaerer continued as I sat patiently while two beautiful red squirrels, one doctor and one nurse, set about fixing my ankles, "the reason I came to see you is that I am concerned that you seem a little to eager to accept the changes that you must make. These changes require much sincerity, dedication and fortitude.

v2020-02-28

"Thank you for your concern, Master Taelbaerer", I replied "I know that you often think of me as a mere child in regards to understanding Saltus Fidelis, the peace that rules and surpasses all understanding, which is due to your national commitment to the One Great God. But I am not a mere Child. In my country, I am considered a rather old man, with many life experiences, many traumas, many losses, many sorrows, and much pain have shaped me to this day. This is why I needed to come to you, to understand a kingdom that was whole, wholesome and holy, and to understand what it meant for me to be whole, holy, and set apart for good works. I have learned so much, but,

"But you live in a government which is not, and can never be ruled by a king, in fact your country was founded on the rejecting the rule of royalty." Added Taelbaerer

"Yes!", I continued, "and how any of these principles apply when your leaders are elected as temporary hired hands that can be put into office and taken back out far too easily.

"Ah," replied Taelbaerer, "we have our Topic of discussion for tomorrow afternoon. I shall take my leave, and see you tomorrow, rest well, obey your doctor.

## OF GOVERNORS AND PRESIDENTS.

(Saturday) The next afternoon, I was met with an oddly subdued gathering. The fact that they had arrived long before I had was not strange, what was strange was their demeanor. For all intents, it appeared that I walked into the middle of a very troubling prayer session. With as much decorum and silence that I was able to maintain as I entered the room, I took my place, and sat down.

Around me, again in very majestic poise and honor, was King Tomek, in full kingly regalia, but not seated on any chair or makeshift throne, but simply seated on his haunches as is the manner of natural squirrels, holding a golden scepter in one paw, and his other paw tightly grasping the paw of Queen Goska seated closely beside him, also seated on her haunches. In Queen Goska's other hand was an intricate lacework towelette.

There was also High Prince Tom, and High Prince Margy, also seating close together, on their haunches, in full regalia. Tom was holding a large scroll, and Margy, who was renowned for her marksmanship, was holding a longbow, and had a full quiver over her shoulder.

Mr. William, entrepreneur and financier and his wife Pearl were seated with Princess Jorie. Princess Jorie wore her classic Germanic Squirrel Princess attire, far more functional than fluffy, but intensely beautiful and designed to accent the best features of the wearer. Mr. William always preferred the fancy pleated pants, shirt, coat and top hat of "Lord Argentarius", which was his bestowed title, given to him by High Princess Margy.

His Wife, Pearl, was wearing a simple but elegant evening gown.

As I surveyed the attire of everyone present, and their deep, pensive and what seemed to be 'lost in prayer' attitudes, my wonderment grew as to what this introduction was all about. Certainly, this was very new to me. Most unexpected.

"Novinaja," began Taelbaerer, "please open this gathering with your convocation."

I presented my prayer convocation as I had in the past few meetings.

"Novinaja", continued Taelbaerer, "each of the members of the court that you see here today, have travelled the lands of your earth many times, doing business, securing treaties, giving counsel, sharing science, and others. Your world is flush with billions of exceptionally bright individuals, who when joined together in marriage or family, become strong"

"But", continued William "whenever they ally themselves into groups larger than a family, they become worse than the dumb beasts of your planet. They scheme how to take from each other, and if that does not work, they gather together to pass laws to punish the industrious, calling them all sorts of defamatory names.

v2020-02-28

"In the past 60 years,", added Madame Pearl, "the most prominent produce that your world has consistently grown, consumed and exported is Anger"

"And now", said King Tomek, "you have asked, how can a person apply the principles of Civil Obedience, as prescribed by your Paul, and desired by King Jesus, in a world ruled by Civil Disobedience."

"and sin", I added.

"I hope that you are making a joke.", said Tomek, "So much Sin today, is taking the ancient writings espousing civil disobedience to the One Great God and saying that *THEY* are preeminent to His scriptures, and therefore you are allowed."

Tomek continued "It is this very notation, from your own Paul, a writing upon which you individuals rise or fall, that we struggle with today.  First, Paul writes this during the time of one of the most self-centered egotistical murderous rulers that human thought has produced, Caesar Nero. Second, Paul does not make any exclusions or limits of obedience or put into place initiatives for civil disobedience should a ruler reach a level of evil, stupidity, self-centeredness, desire to eradicate all of his subjects for his own joy, or ascend to the throne of heaven." Here is what Paul says.

**Let everyone be subject to the governing authorities, for there is no authority except that which God has established.**
**The authorities that exist have been established by God. Consequently, whoever rebels against the authority is rebelling against what God has instituted, and those who do so will bring judgment on themselves.**

King Tomek Then said "You either believe this or you do not. But be warned, disbelief of a saying the One Great God simply because it discomforts you is your bookmark of civil disobedience that will fester and grow in your life against the One Great God and you look back and discover that it began back here.
Then How should you live, as a citizen of your country?

Then Taelbaerer Began:
"First, shall that which impels you to Anger be your sustenance for living, for talking, for loving? Does every conversation need to lead to anger? Too many of those who do NOT follow our King Jesus in your world have anger as their only creative emotion. A follower of Jesus is royalty, a child of the Great God, and does not act like a commoner.

Refuse to let Anger be your governor. It is neither elected, assigned or established to have this right against you.

v2020-02-28

Second. Flee the 'know it all', who engages in conversations only to incite everyone within hearing into anger and frustrations because in the end, no view point can actually change the history of what has happened, or the hearts of persons in power far away and out of your personal reach.

You achieve incredible levels of frustration, because for all the heated talk, anger and evil-wishing, nothing of what you have said has any benefit. Unless, of course, one will actually take good and decent action toward the matter discussed, taking lawful steps to achieve change.

Remember who your elected officials are, and who they are not! While your governors, senators and presidents are appointed to elected offices over you, the media, recording artists, and current social trends were never elected over you, and do not hold office over you. They are not entitled to exercise rule over you, and you are not required to subjugate your thought to them.

If you are a follower of Jesus, then you are Royalty, a citizen first of Heaven. You have a unique paradox not addressed by your country's law's of dual citizenship, nevertheless, your primary ruler is the KING JESUS not the elected official of the time. This does not excuse you from obedience to your rulers, rather it raises you up above the chaos of civil disobedience to be able to easily and without reservation accept your earthly rulers, because you have an accurate assessment of Earth and Heaven."

## SUBJECTS OR SUBJUGATED?

Taelbaerer Continued: In your own reckoning, Novinaja, are you a subject of your King Jesus or have you been merely subjugated, that is, dominated or controlled, by him? Are you a subject of the rulers of the Authorities that the High King God has placed over you on your planet Earth, or are you subjugated and controlled by them?

Taelbaerer continued: "Novinaja, I was once being transported along the West Coast of your United States in a vehicle with several minor diplomats. We were using what was called a "High Occupancy Vehicle" lane or HOV, or "diamond" lane, I think the locals called it. Since we were travelling at a very high rate of speed, while directly alongside of us were several lanes of vehicles stuck in endless traffic, I came up with an interesting idea.

I thought, Perhaps imagine that we are all traveling to meet our king, whose name is *Life, Liberty and the Pursuit of Happiness*. Here in the HOV lane, I am a happy subject of the King, for I have everything. I am in need of nothing, I will be soon praising His benevolence. All the other drivers must feel that they have been subjugated. They know that their king is the giver of Life, Liberty and the Pursuit of Happiness. They will pursue it in sorrow and grief all the days of their short lives, perhaps never really understanding that what they sought is what they had.

Perhaps this is what every one of us means when we end our benediction with "Know God and his Son Jesus". It is not to know of them, and be stuck on the slow lane of knowledge, but to know them well in the fast lane of experience and love.

With that, Taelbaerer sat down, fully relaxed.

v2020-02-28

After pondering for well over an hour, I finally gave my concluding remark for the evening.

"With that last statement, I felt what was like a heavy cloud lifted from the dark places in my heart.

My citizenship in heaven does not excuse me from obedience to my earthy rulers, it raises me above the thousands of years of civil disobedience.
There is nothing forcing me to hate or disobey my rulers, or become embroiled in conversations that breed anger. I can rise above my human DNA and remember that I am now Royalty.

I am able to clearly see the political and spiritual worlds not in conflict, but in symbiosis. If being a follower of Jesus means that I am above the nonsense of sin and shame, all that these lovely squirrels called civil disobedience, then I see the alternatives so much easier.

I can see that while I am on Earth, that I am a 'stranger in a strange land', actually, on mission, to planet Earth, and while I am on mission, I am subject to, and need to carefully obey, its Rulers and Authorities. Even the ones that tend to drive so many others into fits of rage. Also, While I am living here, I am also a missionary, given assigned tasks, whether to teach, help, care for others, disciple, evangelize, preach or more. Whatever talents I have been given, I am to use and grow while on mission on Earth."

v2020-02-28

King Tomek smiled, rose from his seat, the manner of Royal Procession, exited with Queen Goska, followed by High Prince Tom and High Prince Margy.

The next morning, after a very solid and dreamless sleep, I woke up to the slight rapping on the door. It was High Prince Thomas and High Princess Margy.
They were each wearing simpler costumes of the Royalty, not the many layers of coats and capes of the full regalia.
As unseemly as a great Lord and Lady could act, they climbed into my large bed with me, and comfortably sat up.
High Prince Tom first spoke,

"Her Majesty, High Princess Margy and I were very eager to know what all you have learned so far."

That is one trait of all squirrels, royal or common, from Earth or Saltus Fidelis, all share alike: their eagerness, bordering on impatience, is insatiable.

I gathered my thoughts, and sat up in bed. Fortunately, the elegant nighttime wear of silken shirt and trousers that I had been given, were a fine and proper style, to the degree that I was not embarrassed to be reporting to the High Prince and Princess in this manner.

"Lord High Prince Tom and Lady Margy", I began, "You have permitted me to travel with you on many journeys, either through the eyes of the journals of Taelbaerer's books, or in your company. You have exemplified the word 'Lord' in the best ways possible, and yet my eyes could not see it. I only needed to see the love of your people toward you, which I could never do, as long as I assumed that civil disobedience worked in your world as it does in ours."

At this point, Tom and Margy, giggled at the obvious ludicrousness of my statement, and shifted around in their positions.

I continued, "In your reign, as High Prince, I could wish that I was one of your faithful citizens, for I would not delay to give to you the promises of my obedience and fealty. What I have learned is that I already have a Lord, a perfect Lord, a supreme Lord over all of heaven and earth, and that is, of course, my Lord Jesus.

I continued: "I have no need to desire to withhold anything from him, or maintain any references to, or love of, civil disobedience. I simply and purely want to be a follower of His Lordship. I can no longer merely mean "his Lordship in my life", but "my life in His Lordship". Yes, I admit, when I return to Earth very soon, I will be besought on every moment to engage in some act of civil disobedience directly challenging his Lordship in my Life, and I so am grateful for His mercy and forgiveness when I come to his throne, and seek the audience that I know that my Lord gives, when it comes to sorrow and forgiveness."

v2020-02-28

High Princess Margy asked me "are you able to see your Lord, Jesus, crowned, mighty, riding a white horse, ruler of heaven and Earth?"

"Oh yes, oh yes, I see it! Crown him with many crowns!" I blurted out.

I did not realize that many passer-by squirrels had entered my bed-chambers, to listen in to my speech, but with that last comment, there was almost a riot of squirrel tails running all over the room, except for Lord Thomas and Lady Margy, who held their decorum to the last.

"Make Way, Make Way!" came a shout from the back, and into my bedchamber squeezed Taelbaerer and King Tomek who were standing in the back of the crowd, but now demanded to get closer.

Then King Tomek looked around at the large crowd of squirrel folk and his tail chuckled heartily. Then he turned to me and asked.

"I should like to know if you have made your peace with your search for meaning behind your word "King"?

"Oh, King Tomek! The very model of a Lord and King. Compassion, mission, and Justice in your land. Oh Yes, from you, I have learned to close my eyes to my preconceived notions of nepotism and tyranny, and open my eyes to the truth of my God and King who is loving and compassionate, and yet cannot tolerate constant, willful, harmful, civil disobedience.
I Have learned that I am never to pretend that I was hired to be the consults to the king or act the part, the King needs no consultants. The king's actions and outcomes are incontestable and inscrutable by his subjects. This is because he always loves His subjects and can be trusted to the uttermost.

Then king Tomek asked "How do you envision your king, when you say that word?"

I replied "even more so, I look to the visions of the prophets who actually saw God on his Throne. That is the King that I picture."

Tomek reminded me: "But your Lord Jesus is also King, is he not."

I replied, "Yes, and the High King, the Father, put all creation under Jesus dominion. Like you squirrels, I know of the Trinity, I believe in the Three persons, but One God, and cannot explain it, and like you squirrels, and even like Jesus did while he physically walked the Earth, I look for ways for my finite mind to explain it. Jesus spoke of this Father, and also said he was one with his father. I can talk of the High King God, and King Jesus and the Lord Holy Spirit. They are still one.

## TODAY: Peace in Chaos

It has been 6 months since my last visit to Saltus Fidelis and I am told that the next Portal Opening nearest my home will not be for another 18 months. Plenty of time to contemplate, share what I have learned from these marvelous creatures, without giving them direct credit for fear of being thought insane, and to write. At least, when I write, I can fully reveal the stories, the visits, the beauty of the land, the wisdom and orderliness of their society, and their constant mission of goodwill, and most will only think that I am constructing a fantasy.

But what have I learned, what is my "take-away" from my time with Taelbaerer, Tomek, and the other great Squirrels? Have I learned not to say 'Lord', in the same manner that I would say "good morning"? OR every time that I say 'Lord', do I fix the eyes of my imagination on Jesus, the one who took up the cross, and is sitting down at the right hand of the throne of God?

Have I grown to obey the Holy Spirit's guidance in my life, or is the defiant lifestyle of civil disobedience in all other matters drowning out obedience to the Spirit of God?

This is not theology, nor a new revelation, this is simply using stories, as Jesus so often did, to illustrate truth.

I hope you enjoyed it.

## APPENDIX: THE BACKGROUND OF THE BOOK

I am so glad that you have decided to do some research, here in the appendix of the book. This means that you have taken some interest in the background of the land and characters of Saltus Fidelis.

First, Where does Saltus Fidelis fit within the five realms of storytelling? And to that matter, what are the five realms of storytelling? According to library of Saltus Fidelis, the realms of Storytelling are these:

> <u>Reality.</u> Stories which tell of events that happened, or are happening.
> <u>Vision.</u> Stories which tell of events that could happen if certain realities are not changed, and other realities are left unchallenged.
> <u>Fables.</u> Stories that have a moral point, and can use any means of realism or unrealism to portray it.
> <u>Fiction.</u> Stories that have no likelihood of ever happening, but are provided to different age groups with various characters for the pure cause of entertainment.
> <u>Fantasy.</u> This is the realm of Saltus Fidelis and of all stories that have pervaded the human consciousness and bonded with us for millennium. The stories have a life, through the characters and images that have an existence even after you close the book. They are as ageless and timeless as the quest of the Sphinx or galaxies far, far, away.

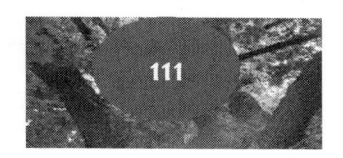

For those who have no knowledge of Saltus Fidelis, and wish to dive deeper into the history, lore and beauty of the land, it is all recorded in the first three volumes, all available on Amazon and Amazon Kindle:

Simply put, a journey to Saltus Fidelis is an encounter with the noble inhabitants of Saltus Fidelis, a world filled with the grace of gallant, honorable and wise squirrels whose sole mission has been to rescue injured or orphaned animals of the Earth, and offer them safe conduct elsewhere on Earth, or a safe haven of peace in Saltus Fidelis.
Although Saltus Fidelis has earned some degree of trust with various groups of Earth animals and humans, there are continuing fears and misgivings of the animals of earth, who are suspicious of the intentions of Saltus Fidelis, believing them to be opportunistic kidnappers and not chivalrous rescuers.

As recorded in the 3rd book on Saltus Fidelis, after the battle to retrieve the stolen property of Saltus Fidelis and rescue a large contingent of the forces of The Free Animals Of the Natural Order Of The Globe Of The Earth, the treaties and trusts between earth animals and Saltus Fidelis are titled the "Oh Faithful Enemy" trusts.

This trust was first described in book 1, during the rescue mission at Tunguska before the meteor blast. Then, as described in book 2, it was hard fought for, with the martyring of Peggy in order to mount a rescue a mission at Mount Saint Helens. Currently "Oh Faithful Enemy" exists as a very specific set of ordinances of when and how aide from Saltus Fidelis is permitted.

The high language of Saltus Fidelis is so similar to our Ancient Latin, that one wonders if one arose from the other.

Saltus Fidelis itself is a term meaning "Faithful Forest", but at the same time it can also mean "Leap of Faith", although to speak such a title is considered currish within her borders.

Whereas the skies and seas of Earth are bathed in blue, the skies and seas of Saltus Fidelis are bathed in Emerald green. A very disorienting difference. Colored sunglasses in the first few months are strongly recommended to support your color sensors in acclimating.

Saltus Fidelis is a world in the shape of a pinwheel, as one would see the Andromeda Galaxy, or imagine the shape of our own Milky way galaxy from afar. Long before entering the world of Physics, planets and worlds in the shapes of globes seemed as implausible to Saltus Fidelis, as a Pin Wheel shape planet would be to earthlings.

Saltus Fidelis is a Monarchy. A single King for many inhabitants. All swearing their loyalty and love without desire for better.

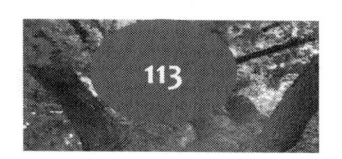

Most of the inhabitants of the Earth, especially those who have become overly educated never really excel in what the Ancients would call Wisdom, and according to many, have gone the way of fools. They cannot accept worlds beyond Physics, and therefore cannot accept the evidences of Fantasy. They do not know of Saltus Fidelis, and only believe what Physics teaches. Their eyes are shut to fantasy and faith. Accordingly, Saltus Fidelis refers to the Great Colliding of Saltus Fidelis and Earth as the intersecting of the World of Fantasy and the World of Physics.

> (The one who holds that the worlds of Physics are the only possible existence, even deny, beyond all evidences, the worlds of Faith, but more on that later.)

Millions of the animal inhabitants of the Earth (and very few humans), who have now transacted with Saltus Fidelis, either as allies, foes, merchants and the millions rescued and given treatments by Saltus Fidelis, have created their own motto. Actually, more of a chant, for it is repeated as a ground-swell until every animal remembers their home "Our Home, and the Free Citizens of the Natural Order of the Globe of the Earth!".

v2020-02-28

I had mentioned earlier the five realms of storytelling, these are quite official according to the libraries of Saltus Fidelis

- The high language of Saltus Fidelis is so similar to our Ancient Latin, that one wonders if one arose from the other.
- Saltus Fidelis itself is a term meaning "Faithful Forest", but at the same time it can also mean "Leap of Faith", although to speak such a title is considered currish within her borders.
- Whereas the skies and seas of Earth are bathed in blue, the skies and seas of Saltus Fidelis are bathed in Emerald green. A very disorienting difference. Colored sunglasses in the first few months are strongly recommended to support your color sensors in acclimating.
- Saltus Fidelis is a world in the shape of a pinwheel, as one would see the Andromeda Galaxy, or imagine the shape of our own Milky way galaxy from afar. Long before entering the world of Physics, planets and worlds in the shapes of globes seemed as implausible to Saltus Fidelis, as a Pin Wheel shape planet would be to earthlings.
- Saltus Fidelis is a Monarchy. A single King for many inhabitants. All swearing their loyalty and love without desire for better.

v2020-02-28

I also should mention something of the Clans of Saltus Fidelis. The Taelbaerers, as a specialized clan, are the most educated, most cultured of all squirrels. Able to converse in in low and high Furorem (the near-Latin languages of Saltus Fidelis), and most of Earth's dialects where squirrels inhabit, they are the teachers and masters to princes and princesses, as well as all common folk. They are seldom known to travel outside of Saltus Fidelis.

The next clan of squirrels, and by far the largest, are called the warrior-poets. From within their ranks arise Lords and Ladies, soldiers, scientists, High Heralds, High dancers, and many similar occupations.

Then come the Gatherers. From the Gather squirrels come workers, builders, scientists, warriors, songsters, low heralds and low dancers, and many other occupations.

In as much as writings, scrolls, manuscripts and books of Saltus Fidelis, the collection of Earth books and antiquities is greater than the libraries of The Library of Ashurbanipal, Alexandria, Pergamum, all of the Dead Sea Scrolls, and the Boston Public Library combined. There were no valuable objects, for that which Saltus Fidelis cherishes as treasure and that which the Earth desires as treasure are of vastly different measures.

It was from this collection of manuscripts that I spent a year studying before bringing my great questions before Taelbaerer, and being told in three simple words "It's all True".

I could go on and on about Saltus Fidelis, there is nothing more that I enjoy talking about. But a low herald squirrel has just summoned me to another meeting with the council. I must not be late.

## Index

| Phrase | Page |
|---|---|
| The world was given Fantasy | 12 |
| The newspapers do an immense amount of thinking for the average man and woman | 18 |
| You mysteriously enjoyed acknowledging that your savior was the express WORD of the ONE GREAT GOD | 26 |
| From the foundations of your people, your earth mother was enticed into an act of civil disobedience against God, simply by doing an action that she was told never to do. It has been written into your DNA ever since. | 29 |
| if a law is a written code but that code is in disobedience to the KING OF KINGS, the Law of the KING OF KINGS supersedes | 30 |
| You feel the freedom to declare to the One Great God that Civil disobedience to HIM is not always sin. | 33 |
| "You have received a gift that many of you do not want because you do not understand your need, that we want more than all the acorns under heaven, but cannot have because we do not need!" | 37 |
| I dreamed I was a butterfly | 41 |
| "Greatness and authority are gifts bestowed on an individual by the One Great God and HE expects each person to use these gifts to lead, to guide, to protect and reassure. | 52 |

v2020-02-28

# Index

| Phrase | Page |
|---|---|
| "What a buffoon I can be with Jesus". | 53 |
| what stands between all men and their understanding and desire for their Lord and King is their narrow Vision, and man's reckless desire to put God into a box of their own understanding. | 57 |
| I am certain that a Lord who claims hereditary right or preeminence to wield the title, must have proven his worthiness to become a Lord through a quest that will demonstrate his compassion, service and sacrifice. | 67 |
| We all exist, that is the fact. The GIFT, is that we are each called to live well. | 74 |
| Trust is like a great bridge held up by huge cables, securing long spans between persons | |

# Bibliography

Saltus Fidelis:
History of our Land by Taelbaerer the First: First Age, Books I-IV
Saltus Fidelis and the Incident at Mt Saint Helens, Amazon, 2017
Great Poems and Greater Poets, Books xviii-cxc
Trade Document depository, Earth years 2000bc – 2000ad
Animals of Earth, care, treatment, habitats
**Treaties:**
    The Dragons Gate: 6207 BC, Mutual Defense Actions
    The Taylor-Polk Accords, 1849. Fair Trade Act with United States
    The Jenkinson Accords, 1819, Fair Trade Act with Great British (Empire)
    The Hallstein Accords, 1965, Fair Trade with European Commission
    Faithful Enemy Act: 2010, Treaty with *The Free Animals of the Natural Order of the Globe of the Earth (FANOGOE)*, allowing continued access for missions of mercy and commerce.

Earth:
The Holy Bible: Writings of Isaiah, Writings of Ezekiel, Gospel of Matthew, Gospel of John, Letter to the Romans, The Revelation of Jesus Christ given to John.
C.S. Lewis: The abolition of Man, The Chronicles of Narnia
Pliney the Elder, writings
Aristotle, writings
Socrates, writings

## Your Memoirs

v2020-02-28

Made in the USA
Columbia, SC
28 February 2020